Understanding the Constitution

Understanding
the Constitution

EDWARD S. CORWIN

McCormick Professor Emeritus of Jurisprudence
Princeton University

AND

JACK W. PELTASON

Assistant Professor of Government
Smith College

WILLIAM SLOANE ASSOCIATES, INC.

Publishers - - - - - - - - - *New York*

16046

Contents

Preface

The Constitution of the United States, the supreme law of our land, is by no means self-explanatory. In an attempt to make it understandable, this brief book sets forth the main features of the Constitution and the practical significance of its most important provisions as they are construed and applied today.

Each Article of the Constitution is taken up section by section and explained, amplified, and interpreted in non-technical terms for both the beginning student and the layman.

If this modest volume succeeds in giving its readers a clear understanding of the document itself and an appreciation of the important role which constitutional interpretation plays in the conduct of our government, it will be fulfilling its purpose.

E. S. C., Princeton, N. J.
J. W. P., Northampton, Mass.

May, 1949.

The Preamble

W E THE PEOPLE OF THE UNITED STATES, IN ORDER TO
FORM A MORE PERFECT UNION, ESTABLISH JUSTICE,
INSURE DOMESTIC TRANQUILITY, PROVIDE FOR THE COM-
MON DEFENSE, PROMOTE THE GENERAL WELFARE, AND
SECURE THE BLESSINGS OF LIBERTY TO OURSELVES AND
OUR POSTERITY, DO ORDAIN AND ESTABLISH THIS CONSTI-
TUTION FOR THE UNITED STATES OF AMERICA.

The Preamble is the prologue of the Constitution. It pro-
claims the source of the Constitution's authority and the great
ends to be accomplished under it.

From the Preamble we learn that the Constitution claims
obedience, not simply because of its intrinsic excellence or the
merit of its principles, but because it is ordained and established
by the people. "The government of the Union," said Chief
Justice Marshall, " . . . is emphatically and truly, a government of the people. In form, and in substance, it emanates from
them. Its powers are granted by them, and are to be exercised
directly on them, and for their benefit."[1] The people are the
masters of the Constitution—not the reverse.

Article I—The Legislative Article

Section 1

ALL LEGISLATIVE POWERS HEREIN GRANTED SHALL BE VESTED IN A CONGRESS OF THE UNITED STATES, WHICH SHALL CONSIST OF A SENATE AND A HOUSE OF REPRESENTATIVES.

The powers and duties of Congress, the President, and the courts are set forth in separate articles, making it clear that the writers of the Constitution intended to prevent a concentration of all powers in the hands of any one department. There is often, nevertheless, a blending of powers, and each department has at least some control over the acts of the other departments. In short, the total power of the national government is divided, and the separated powers frequently check one another (see pages 17–18, 35–36, 64–66).

It is significant that of the three branches of the national government the legislative branch is mentioned first. The framers of the Constitution desired "a government of laws and not of men,"[1] and in normal times expected Congress to be the central and directing organ of the government within the field of its delegated powers. War and Emergency would, of course, be a different matter (see pages 47–48).

It was also a maxim with the framers that "the legislature may not delegate its powers,"[2] but in recent years, the force of this principle has declined in the face of the complexity and changeableness of the conditions which Congress is often called upon to regulate. Nowadays it is sufficient if Congress enacts in clear terms *a general policy*. Once it has done this, it may authorize administrative officials to make rules designed to carry such policy into effect. Thus, Congress cannot effectively supervise railroad rate making on the thousands of commodities which are transported between the thousands of places in the United States, wherefore it has established the general policy that rates must be "fair and reasonable" and has delegated to the Interstate Commerce Commission the responsibility for applying this rule in individual cases. Likewise Congress had power to set up the Federal Power Commission and authorize it to determine "just and reasonable rates" for the sale of natural gas in interstate commerce; to establish a Federal Communications Commission and authorize it to regulate radio broadcasting in the "public interest, convenience, or necessity"; to establish a Federal Trade Commission and authorize it to prevent "unfair methods of competition" in interstate commerce; and so on.[3]

With one very important exception Congress has no legislative powers except those "herein granted" by the Constitution. Powers not granted or powers which cannot reasonably be implied from the granted powers are denied to Congress and reserved to the states (see Amendment Ten, page 105). By way of contrast, the British Parliament has complete legislative powers over all matters.

The field of foreign relations provides the exception just mentioned to the above general rule. As "necessary concomitants of nationality," the Supreme Court has said, the national government would have full power with respect to the external relations of the United States even though the subject were not mentioned in the Constitution. The power to acquire territory by discovery and occupation, the power to make international agreements which are not treaties in a constitutional sense, *the power to wage war*, are not among the powers which are specifically granted by the Constitution to the national government; they are *powers inherent in its national character*. For the source and scope of such powers one must turn to international law and practice, not to the Constitution. As a member of the

Except Those

· 3 ·

Society of Nations, the United States has as great powers as any other nation in the field of external relations.[4]

By granting legislative powers to two distinct branches of Congress, a bicameral (two-chamber) legislature was created, as contrasted with a single-chamber or unicameral legislature. Of the framers only Benjamin Franklin favored a single-chamber legislature. The others felt that two chambers were needed so that representation in one might be based on population, while in the other the states would be represented as states and hence equally. Also, it was thought, the two chambers would serve as a check upon each other and so often prevent the passage of ill-considered or oppressive legislation.

Section 2

1. THE HOUSE OF REPRESENTATIVES SHALL BE COM-
POSED OF MEMBERS CHOSEN EVERY SECOND YEAR BY
THE PEOPLE OF THE SEVERAL STATES, AND THE ELEC-
TORS IN EACH STATE SHALL HAVE THE QUALIFICA-
TIONS REQUISITE FOR ELECTORS OF THE MOST NUMER-
OUS BRANCH OF THE STATE LEGISLATURE.

The word "electors" in this paragraph means voters. In 1787 voting qualifications varied more widely from state to state than they do today. In the Constitutional Convention an overwhelming majority of the delegates believed that the suffrage should be limited to those who had some kind of property, but since they could not agree as to the amount or kind of property that should be required, it was finally left for the individual states to determine the qualifications of voters for representatives, who were the only members of the national government that the framers intended the voters should choose directly.

Subject to Amendments Fourteen, Fifteen, and Nineteen (see pages 116–126, 132–133) the several states still fix the suffrage qualifications. The right to vote in a federal election is, never-theless, a right conferred by the Constitution—in the above provision, to wit—and the national government accordingly has power to protect the voter in the exercise of this right against private fraud or violence and against state discrimination.[5]

Section 2

2. NO PERSON SHALL BE A REPRESENTATIVE WHO SHALL NOT HAVE ATTAINED TO THE AGE OF TWENTY FIVE YEARS, AND BEEN SEVEN YEARS A CITIZEN OF THE UNITED STATES, AND WHO SHALL NOT, WHEN ELECTED, BE AN INHABITANT OF THE STATE IN WHICH HE SHALL BE CHOSEN.

In other words, persons who are twenty-five years or over, who have been citizens of the United States for seven years, and who are citizens of the state which they represent are constitutionally eligible for membership in the House of Representatives. The remaining prerequisites are election by the voters and acceptance by the House (see pages 12–13).

Although the Constitution does not require a member of Congress to reside in the district which he represents, politically it is almost essential since the voters refuse to elect a non-resident. By way of contrast, under British practice members of Parliament are often elected to represent districts other than those in which they live. Our insistence upon local residence leads to some unfortunate results. As the late Charles Beard once said, brains are not geographically distributed. The local-residence rule prevents the less fortunate districts from benefiting from the overflow of talents from the more fortunate districts. It also reflects and supports the too prevalent belief that a representative's primary obligation is to his own district rather than to the country as a whole, an attitude which has often deterred congressmen from thinking nationally and has compelled them to seek "pap" in the form of appropriations and jobs for their districts regardless of the effect on national policy or interests.

Section 2

3. REPRESENTATIVES AND DIRECT TAXES SHALL BE AP-
PORTIONED AMONG THE SEVERAL STATES WHICH MAY
BE INCLUDED WITHIN THIS UNION, ACCORDING TO
THEIR RESPECTIVE NUMBERS, WHICH SHALL BE DE-
TERMINED BY ADDING TO THE WHOLE NUMBER OF
FREE PERSONS, INCLUDING THOSE BOUND TO SERVICE
FOR A TERM OF YEARS, AND EXCLUDING INDIANS NOT
TAXED, THREE FIFTHS OF ALL OTHER PERSONS.

The term "other persons" meant slaves. Thanks to Amendment XIII, Amendment XIV, Section 2, and Amendment XVI,
this paragraph is today practically obsolete.

Section 2

3. continued: THE ACTUAL ENUMERATION SHALL BE
MADE WITHIN THREE YEARS AFTER THE FIRST MEET-
ING OF THE CONGRESS OF THE UNITED STATES, AND
WITHIN EVERY SUBSEQUENT TERM OF TEN YEARS,
IN SUCH MANNER AS THEY SHALL BY LAW DIRECT.
THE NUMBER OF REPRESENTATIVES SHALL NOT EX-
CEED ONE FOR EVERY THIRTY THOUSAND, BUT EACH
STATE SHALL HAVE AT LEAST ONE REPRESENTATIVE;

This restriction on the size of the House of Representatives
is today obsolete. Since our present population stands at approximately 145 million, this limit would allow of 4,833 members (145 million divided by 30,000). Obviously a chamber
of this size would be of little value, and Congress has limited
by law the number of representatives to 435, approximately
one representative for every 300,000 persons. These 435 are
distributed among the states according to population as nearly
as possible. The number of inhabitants, however, that a particular congressman may represent varies widely. This results
from several things: (1) the fact that every state regardless
of population is entitled to one representative—three states,
Nevada, Wyoming, and Delaware each have less than 300,000 in-

habitants; (2) population movements into or out of congressional districts; (3) the frequent failure of state legislatures to redistrict their states; and (4) their failure to establish approximately equal congressional districts. Although Congress determines the number of representatives to which each state is entitled on the basis of its population, it is for the state legislatures to divide their respective states into congressional districts, each of which elects one representative. In many cases the determination of congressional districts is influenced by partisan considerations. The party in control of the state legislature generally tries to carve up the state in such a way that the voters of the opposite party are concentrated in as few districts as possible, a practice which is known as "gerrymandering."

Section 2

3. continued: AND UNTIL SUCH ENUMERATION SHALL BE MADE, THE STATE OF NEW HAMPSHIRE SHALL BE ENTITLED TO CHOOSE THREE, MASSACHUSETTS EIGHT, RHODE-ISLAND AND PROVIDENCE PLANTATIONS ONE, CONNECTICUT FIVE, NEW YORK SIX, NEW JERSEY FOUR, PENNSYLVANIA EIGHT, DELAWARE ONE, MARYLAND SIX, VIRGINIA TEN, NORTH CAROLINA FIVE, SOUTH CAROLINA FIVE, AND GEORGIA THREE.

This was a temporary provision until a census could be taken to determine the basis of representation. It has no significance today.

Section 2

4. WHEN VACANCIES HAPPEN IN THE REPRESENTATION FROM ANY STATE, THE EXECUTIVE AUTHORITY THEREOF SHALL ISSUE WRITS OF ELECTION TO FILL SUCH VACANCIES.

5. THE HOUSE OF REPRESENTATIVES SHALL CHOOSE THEIR SPEAKER AND OTHER OFFICERS; AND SHALL HAVE THE SOLE POWER OF IMPEACHMENT.

In form, the Speaker of the House is chosen by the House of Representatives; in fact, he is chosen by the majority party, or more precisely, by a majority of the majority party. The duties and powers of the Speaker and of the other officers are determined by the rules and practices of the House. Curiously enough, the Constitution does not specify that the Speaker must be a member of the House. The framers simply assumed that the example of the British House of Commons and of the state assemblies would be followed.

"Power of impeachment" means the power to accuse and to bring formal charges against a person. It is a common error to think that the power to impeach means the power to remove a person from office; in fact, it is only the first step in that direction (see pages 10–11, 54–55).

Section 3

1. THE SENATE OF THE UNITED STATES SHALL BE COM-POSED OF TWO SENATORS FROM EACH STATE, CHOSEN BY THE LEGISLATURE THEREOF, FOR SIX YEARS; AND EACH SENATOR SHALL HAVE ONE VOTE.

The underlined portion of this section has been superseded by the Seventeenth Amendment (see pages 128–129).

The framers adopted equal representation of all states in the Senate at the insistence of the smaller states, who made it their price for accepting the Constitution. As a result of their victory, the 110,000 inhabitants of Nevada and the 250,000 inhabitants of Wyoming have the same number of representatives in the Senate as do the 13,000,000 inhabitants of New York and the 10,000,000 of California. It means that the New England States with 6.4 per cent of the total population have 12.5 per cent of the Senate seats, while the Mountain States with only 3.1 per cent of the total population have 16.6 per cent. On the other hand, the Middle Atlantic States with 20.9 per cent of the total population have only 6.2 per cent of the Senate seats and the East North Central States with 20.2 per cent of the total population have only 10.4 per cent.[6] These figures account for the disproportionate influence which the mining and agricultural interests, and especially the former, have sometimes exerted through the Senate upon legislation.

Section 3

2. IMMEDIATELY AFTER THEY SHALL BE ASSEMBLED IN CONSEQUENCE OF THE FIRST ELECTION, THEY SHALL BE DIVIDED AS EQUALLY AS MAY BE INTO THREE CLASSES. THE SEATS OF THE SENATORS OF THE FIRST CLASS SHALL BE VACATED AT THE EXPIRATION OF THE SECOND YEAR, OF THE SECOND CLASS AT THE EXPIRATION OF THE FOURTH YEAR, AND OF THE THIRD CLASS AT THE EXPIRATION OF THE SIXTH YEAR, SO THAT ONE THIRD MAY BE CHOSEN EVERY SECOND YEAR;

As a result of this original division of senators into three classes, the Senate has been a continuous body. Only one third of the senators' terms expire at the same time; hence at least two thirds of its members at any time have been members of the preceding Congress.

Section 3

2. continued: AND IF VACANCIES HAPPEN BY RESIGNATION, OR OTHERWISE, DURING THE RECESS OF THE LEGISLATURE OF ANY STATE, THE EXECUTIVE THEREOF MAY MAKE TEMPORARY APPOINTMENTS UNTIL THE NEXT MEETING OF THE LEGISLATURE, WHICH SHALL THEN FILL SUCH VACANCIES.

This section was modified by the Seventeenth Amendment which provides for the direct election of senators. (See page 128).

Section 3

3. NO PERSON SHALL BE A SENATOR WHO SHALL NOT HAVE ATTAINED TO THE AGE OF THIRTY YEARS, AND BEEN NINE YEARS A CITIZEN OF THE UNITED STATES,

AND WHO SHALL NOT, WHEN ELECTED, BE AN INHABI-
TANT OF THAT STATE FOR WHICH HE SHALL BE
CHOSEN.

(See page 13.)

Section 3

4. THE VICE PRESIDENT OF THE UNITED STATES SHALL
BE PRESIDENT OF THE SENATE, BUT SHALL HAVE NO
VOTE, UNLESS THEY BE EQUALLY DIVIDED.

The Vice-President has much less control over the Senate
than the Speaker has over the House. For example, he must
recognize senators in the order in which they rise and ask for
recognition, while the Speaker has discretionary powers in rec-
ognizing members from the floor. These and other differences
grow out of congressional customs and usages and do not stem
from the Constitution.

The first Vice-President, John Adams, exercised his "casting
vote" some twenty times, a record that still stands.

Section 3

5. THE SENATE SHALL CHOOSE THEIR OTHER OFFICERS,
AND ALSO A PRESIDENT PRO TEMPORE, IN THE ABSENCE
OF THE VICE PRESIDENT, OR WHEN HE SHALL EXER-
CISE THE OFFICE OF PRESIDENT OF THE UNITED STATES.

The President pro tempore of the Senate is chosen by the
majority party. He is normally the member of the majority
party with the longest continuous service in the Senate. Unlike
the Vice-President, he can, being a senator, vote on any and
every matter before the Senate.

Section 3

6. THE SENATE SHALL HAVE THE SOLE POWER TO TRY
ALL IMPEACHMENTS.

When the House of Representatives impeaches a federal officer, he is tried before the Senate.

Section 3

6. continued: WHEN SITTING FOR THAT PURPOSE, THEY SHALL BE ON OATH OR AFFIRMATION. WHEN THE PRESIDENT OF THE UNITED STATES IS TRIED THE CHIEF JUSTICE SHALL PRESIDE: AND NO PERSON SHALL BE CONVICTED WITHOUT THE CONCURRENCE OF TWO THIRDS OF THE MEMBERS PRESENT.

The House has impeached twelve civil officers of the United States, of whom the Senate has convicted only four. Although Supreme Court Justice Samuel Chase (1802) and President Andrew Johnson (1868) were impeached, the Senate failed to sustain the charges against them; all of those convicted by the Senate were judges of the inferior federal courts. Several officers, however, have resigned to escape impeachment or trial.

Section 3

7. JUDGMENT IN CASES OF IMPEACHMENT SHALL NOT EXTEND FURTHER THAN TO REMOVAL FROM OFFICE, AND DISQUALIFICATIONS TO HOLD AND ENJOY ANY OFFICE OF HONOR, TRUST OR PROFIT UNDER THE UNITED STATES: BUT THE PARTY CONVICTED SHALL NEVERTHELESS BE LIABLE AND SUBJECT TO INDICTMENT, TRIAL, JUDGMENT AND PUNISHMENT, ACCORDING TO LAW.

(See pages 7–8, 54–55.)

Section 4

1. THE TIMES, PLACES AND MANNER OF HOLDING ELECTIONS FOR SENATORS AND REPRESENTATIVES, SHALL BE PRESCRIBED IN EACH STATE BY THE LEGISLATURE THEREOF; BUT THE CONGRESS MAY AT ANY TIME BY

LAW MAKE OR ALTER SUCH REGULATIONS, EXCEPT AS
TO THE PLACES OF CHOOSING SENATORS.

Congress has established the first Tuesday after the first Monday in November in the even-numbered years as the date for the election of senators and representatives, except when other times are prescribed by state constitutions. Nowadays the exception applies only to Maine, whose constitution prescribes the second Monday in September as the time for holding elections for United States senators and representatives. "As Maine goes, so goes the nation"—sometimes.

Congress requires that the district system be used for the election of representatives (see pages 6–7), and that elections be by secret ballot. Also Congress has placed a limit on the expenditures of candidates seeking election to Congress and has taken steps to prevent corrupt and fraudulent practices in connection with these elections. The Supreme Court has recently interpreted the word "elections" to include primaries in which candidates for the Senate and House are nominated, if such primaries effectively control the choice, as is generally the case in several Southern states.[7] Congressional power as to time, places, and manner consequently extends to such primaries.

Section 4

2. THE CONGRESS SHALL ASSEMBLE AT LEAST ONCE IN
EVERY YEAR, AND SUCH MEETING SHALL BE ON THE
FIRST MONDAY IN DECEMBER, UNLESS THEY SHALL BY
LAW APPOINT A DIFFERENT DAY.

The Twentieth Amendment has superseded this paragraph. (See page 134).

Section 5

1. EACH HOUSE SHALL BE THE JUDGE OF THE ELECTIONS,
RETURNS AND QUALIFICATIONS OF ITS OWN MEMBERS,

The Constitution, as we have seen, lists the qualifications for membership in the House of Representatives and the Senate. It might seem to follow that the power of each house to judge the qualifications of its own members would merely comprise the right to determine whether a particular member has these stipulated qualifications and that neither house, or even Congress, would have the power to add to this list. (See pages 5, 9–10.) As a matter of fact, both the House and the Senate have at times denied duly elected and constitutionally qualified persons their seats because they were morally or politically objectionable to a majority of the respective chambers. Thus the House in 1900 refused to admit Brigham H. Roberts from Utah because he was a polygamist and, in the opinion of a majority, morally unfit. A more extreme case was that of Victor L. Berger who was twice elected by his constituents in Wisconsin, but twice excluded from the House because of his purported "un-American" beliefs. The Senate too has at times added to the qualifications of senators-elect and refused them their seats. Such precedents, which spring in the first instance from the practice of the British Parliament and the early state legislatures, open the way for a majority in either house to deprive the people of a congressional district or of a state of representation on purely political or doctrinal grounds.

Section 5

1. continued: AND A MAJORITY OF EACH [house] SHALL CONSTITUTE A QUORUM TO DO BUSINESS; BUT A SMALLER NUMBER MAY ADJOURN FROM DAY TO DAY, AND MAY BE AUTHORIZED TO COMPEL THE ATTENDANCE OF ABSENT MEMBERS, IN SUCH MANNER, AND UNDER SUCH PENALTIES AS EACH HOUSE MAY PROVIDE.

2. EACH HOUSE MAY DETERMINE THE RULES OF ITS PROCEEDINGS, PUNISH ITS MEMBERS FOR DISORDERLY BEHAVIOR, AND, WITH THE CONCURRENCE OF TWO THIRDS, EXPEL A MEMBER.

Although it takes only a majority, that is the majority of a quorum, to prevent a member-elect from being seated, it takes two thirds of a quorum to expel a member once he has been admitted to membership, "seated," that is. Since congressmen are not liable to impeachment, expulsion by their respective chambers is the only way they may be unseated—except, of course, by defeat at the polls.

Section 5

3. EACH HOUSE SHALL KEEP A JOURNAL OF ITS PROCEED-INGS, AND FROM TIME TO TIME PUBLISH THE SAME, EXCEPTING SUCH PARTS AS MAY IN THEIR JUDGMENT REQUIRE SECRECY; AND THE YEAS AND NAYS OF THE MEMBERS OF EITHER HOUSE ON ANY QUESTION SHALL, AT THE DESIRE OF ONE FIFTH OF THOSE PRESENT, BE ENTERED ON THE JOURNAL.

This is consistent with the belief that in a republic the proceedings of the legislature should be published except in unusual circumstances.

The *Journal* should not be confused with the *Congressional Record*. The *Journal* is the official record of congressional acts, resolutions, votes, etc., whereas the *Record* pretends to be a report of what is *said* in each house. In fact, because of the practice of freely allowing members to "revise and extend their remarks," as well as to print articles, speeches, poems, and so on by non-members, much appears in the *Congressional Record* that was never said on the floors of Congress and would be more suitable in a popular magazine.

By the parliamentary device of resolving itself into a Committee of the Whole, the House of Representatives can avoid the constitutional necessity of a roll-call vote on the demand of a fifth of those present. On the other hand, when the House of Representatives is in session, a minority by demanding a roll call, which takes between thirty and forty-five minutes, has a weapon to defend itself against a "steam-rolling" majority. Mechanical devices exist, however, by which the roll could nowadays be taken in a fraction of this time.

Section 5

4. NEITHER HOUSE, DURING THE SESSION OF CONGRESS, SHALL, WITHOUT THE CONSENT OF THE OTHER, ADJOURN FOR MORE THAN THREE DAYS, NOR TO ANY OTHER PLACE THAN THAT IN WHICH THE TWO HOUSES SHALL BE SITTING.

In addition to the above powers each house enjoys important powers by inheritance, as it were, from the English Parliament and the early state legislatures. Their power to exclude persons from membership is one of these, as we have seen. A very important one is their power to create committees with authority to conduct investigations into subjects on which they may wish to legislate. Such committees—the House Committee on Un-American Activities, for example—have the power to summon and examine witnesses, and to report recalcitrant witnesses for punishment for "contempt."[8] Also, each house can punish outsiders who interrupt its proceedings for "contempt."

Section 6

1. THE SENATORS AND REPRESENTATIVES SHALL RECEIVE A COMPENSATION FOR THEIR SERVICES, TO BE ASCERTAINED BY LAW, AND PAID OUT OF THE TREASURY OF THE UNITED STATES.

Although elected by the people of the states or congressional districts, it is to the national treasury that congressmen must look for their compensation. During the struggle for ratification of the Constitution many persons had objected to this provision because it permitted congressmen to determine their own salaries. Actually, congressmen have been reluctant to increase their salaries or even to set them at a figure high enough to permit persons without other sources of income to serve in Congress without financial embarrassment. The financial demands on a congressman are great; he must ordinarily maintain two residences and meet many political and social obligations. At the present time congressmen receive a yearly salary of $12,500 plus an allowance of $2,500, of which only the former is subject to the income tax.

Section 6

1. continued: THEY SHALL IN ALL CASES, EXCEPT TREASON, FELONY, AND BREACH OF THE PEACE, BE PRIVILEGED FROM ARREST DURING THEIR ATTENDANCE AT THE SESSION OF THEIR RESPECTIVE HOUSES, AND IN GOING TO AND RETURNING FROM THE SAME;

Congressmen are granted this privilege to protect them from interference in the pursuit of their duties. They are not exempt from the obligations of the laws, from the jurisdiction of the courts, or from summons in civil cases. The exemption extends only to *arrest* for minor offenses while engaged in congressional business.

Section 6

1. continued: AND FOR ANY SPEECH OR DEBATE IN EITHER HOUSE, THEY SHALL NOT BE QUESTIONED IN ANY OTHER PLACE.

This privilege is much broader than the one mentioned above. Congressmen are exempt from arrest, prosecution, or suit for anything they say on the floors of Congress or in committee, or in committee reports, regardless of how libelous, slanderous, or seditious it may be.

Section 6

2. NO SENATOR OR REPRESENTATIVE SHALL, DURING THE TIME FOR WHICH HE WAS ELECTED, BE APPOINTED TO ANY CIVIL OFFICE UNDER THE AUTHORITY OF THE UNITED STATES, WHICH SHALL HAVE BEEN CREATED, OR THE EMOLUMENTS WHEREOF SHALL HAVE BEEN INCREASED DURING SUCH TIME; AND NO PERSON HOLDING ANY OFFICE UNDER THE UNITED STATES, SHALL

BE A MEMBER OF EITHER HOUSE DURING HIS CON-
TINUANCE IN OFFICE.

A member of Congress may not serve in the executive branch
of the government and retain his membership in Congress. This
rule, which stems from the doctrine of separation of powers,
contrasts sharply with the British system where most high executive ministers are members of Parliament. But the rule does
not prevent the appointment of congressmen as temporary representatives of the United States at international conferences.
For example, Senator Vandenberg was a member of the United
States delegation to the San Francisco United Nations Confer-
ence and yet continued to be a United States senator. Also,
there is no constitutional prohibition against a congressman
serving as a state officer, but the situation seldom arises, there
seldom being enough offices to go around.

Section 7

> 1. ALL BILLS FOR RAISING REVENUE SHALL ORIGINATE IN
> THE HOUSE OF REPRESENTATIVES; BUT THE SENATE
> MAY PROPOSE OR CONCUR WITH AMENDMENTS AS ON
> OTHER BILLS.

This provision is based on the theory that the House is more
directly responsive to the will of the people than the Senate,
and was inserted in the Constitution at the insistence of the more
populous states, in order to tie up taxation with representation.
It has not, however, kept the Senate in fact from originating
revenue measures in the guise of amending House bills, by strik-
ing out an entire measure except the title and the enacting clause.
This paragraph, moreover, does not have the same significance
that it had in 1787, when senators were chosen by state
legislatures.

Section 7

> 2. EVERY BILL WHICH SHALL HAVE PASSED THE HOUSE
> OF REPRESENTATIVES AND THE SENATE, SHALL, BEFORE

IT BECOME A LAW, BE PRESENTED TO THE PRESIDENT OF THE UNITED STATES; IF HE APPROVES HE SHALL SIGN IT, BUT IF NOT HE SHALL RETURN IT, WITH HIS OBJECTIONS TO THAT HOUSE IN WHICH IT SHALL HAVE ORIGINATED, WHO SHALL ENTER THE OBJECTIONS AT LARGE ON THEIR JOURNAL, AND PROCEED TO RECONSIDER IT. IF AFTER SUCH RECONSIDERATION TWO THIRDS OF THAT HOUSE SHALL AGREE TO PASS THE BILL, IT SHALL BE SENT, TOGETHER WITH THE OBJECTIONS, TO THE OTHER HOUSE, BY WHICH IT SHALL LIKEWISE BE RECONSIDERED, AND IF APPROVED BY TWO THIRDS OF THAT HOUSE, IT SHALL BECOME A LAW. BUT IN ALL SUCH CASES THE VOTES OF BOTH HOUSES SHALL BE DETERMINED BY YEAS AND NAYS, AND THE NAMES OF THE PERSONS VOTING FOR AND AGAINST THE BILL SHALL BE ENTERED ON THE JOURNAL OF EACH HOUSE RESPECTIVELY. IF ANY BILL SHALL NOT BE RETURNED BY THE PRESIDENT WITHIN TEN DAYS (SUNDAYS EXCEPTED) AFTER IT SHALL HAVE BEEN PRESENTED TO HIM, THE SAME SHALL BE A LAW, IN LIKE MANNER AS IF HE HAD SIGNED IT, UNLESS THE CONGRESS BY THEIR ADJOURNMENT PREVENTED ITS RETURN, IN WHICH CASE IT SHALL NOT BE A LAW.

While the framers expected Congress to be the dominant branch of the government, they did not wish it to be in position to arrogate to itself all powers. So they gave the President a qualified veto both to prevent Congress from overstepping its boundaries, and to enable him to influence the actual course of legislation.

After a bill has been passed in *identical* form by both houses of Congress, it is presented to the President, who can do one of three things:

First, if he approves, he can sign the bill and it becomes the law of the land.

Second, if he does not approve, he can return it to the house in which it originated, stating the reasons for his disapproval.

If the bill is then repassed by a two-thirds vote of *both* houses, which means two thirds of a quorum of the members thereof, it becomes law despite the President's veto. On the other hand, if the bill does not secure the approval of two thirds of a quorum of the members of *both* houses, the veto is sustained and the bill does not become law.

Third, the President can refuse to sign the bill, but retain possession of it. It then becomes law at the end of ten days (excluding Sundays) after being presented to him *if Congress is still in session*. But if Congress adjourns before the lapse of the ten days (excluding Sundays), the bill does not become law, in which case it is a victim of what is known as a "pocket veto." Congresses have occasionally remained in session until ten days have elapsed in order to prevent the President from thus defeating their measures.

Unlike many state governors, the President cannot approve parts of a bill and veto other parts; he must give his approval or disapproval to the bill as a single unit. Because the President does not have an "item veto," Congress has been able to get measures past the President by using "riders," a term for provisions which are not germane to the main purpose of a bill. Riders are most effective when tacked on to appropriation bills, thus forcing the President to accept them in order to secure funds for the operations of the government. Despite the attempts of the Legislative Reorganization Act of 1946 to discourage it, this practice still continues.

Section 7

3. EVERY ORDER, RESOLUTION, OR VOTE TO WHICH THE CONCURRENCE OF THE SENATE AND HOUSE OF REPRESENTATIVES MAY BE NECESSARY (EXCEPT ON A QUESTION OF ADJOURNMENT) SHALL BE PRESENTED TO THE PRESIDENT OF THE UNITED STATES; AND BEFORE THE SAME SHALL TAKE EFFECT, SHALL BE APPROVED BY HIM, OR BEING DISAPPROVED BY HIM, SHALL BE REPASSED BY TWO THIRDS OF THE SENATE AND HOUSE OF REPRESENTATIVES, ACCORDING TO THE

Despite the inclusive language of this section there are, in addition to questions of adjournment, certain orders, resolutions, and votes which require the concurrence of both houses, but are not presented to the President.

When a constitutional amendment is proposed by a two-thirds vote of both houses of Congress, that is by a vote of two thirds of a quorum thereof, it is submitted immediately for ratification without being sent to the President for his approval or disapproval. Congress does not exercise ordinary legislative powers when it proposes constitutional amendments, but operates under the powers given it in Article V (see page 74). This is a self-contained, complete statement of methods for amending the Constitution and omits the President from the amending procedure.

The second exception is the "concurrent resolution." This formerly was not legislation, but merely gave expression to congressional sentiments or opinions, for the most part. But recently a more important use has been found for it in connection with laws delegating powers to the President. By stipulating in the original law that the powers delegated may be rescinded by "concurrent resolution," the President is denied the opportunity to use his veto and thus to require a two-thirds vote to withdraw powers which were granted him by a majority.

This use of the concurrent resolution has been criticized as an evasion of Article I, Section 7, but there can be little doubt that Congress will continue to use it in this fashion. The development of this practice is an excellent example of congressional constitutional interpretation.

Section 8

Section 8 enumerates the powers granted to Congress. In interpreting these powers we should never, as Chief Justice Marshall put it, forget that it is a *Constitution* we are reading, a Constitution which was "intended to endure for ages to come, and, consequently, to be adapted to the various *crises* of human affairs."[9] Furthermore, each separate enumerated grant should be read as if paragraph 18 of the Section (see page 32) was a part of it.

Section 8

1. THE CONGRESS SHALL HAVE POWER TO LAY AND COL-
   LECT TAXES, DUTIES, IMPOSTS AND EXCISES, TO PAY
   THE DEBTS AND PROVIDE FOR THE COMMON DEFENSE
   AND GENERAL WELFARE OF THE UNITED STATES;

This paragraph grants to Congress the important power of the purse. A word of caution—Congress does not have the power to legislate generally for the general welfare; it has the power only *to tax and spend* for the general welfare. The "general welfare" clause is tied inextricably to the power to tax and spend. Otherwise the specific enumeration of other congressional powers would be superfluous.

James Madison argued in vain that Congress could tax and spend only in order to carry out one of its other granted powers, that is, Congress could tax and spend only to establish post offices and post roads (Section 8, (7)), to regulate commerce with foreign nations (Section 8, (3)), and so forth. From the first, nevertheless, the power of Congress under this clause has been interpreted as being *in addition* to its other powers, and hence as exercisable in its own right without reference to them. Today Congress taxes and spends hundreds of millions every year to aid agriculture, education, business, to alleviate conditions of unemployment, to promote low-cost housing, despite the fact that none of these things are specifically within its other delegated powers.

This power is consequently one of the two major sources of the so-called "national police power." By "police power" is meant the power to regulate persons and property for the safety, health, and welfare of society. Although Congress has no general grant of "police power," it has been able, through its authority to tax and spend for the general welfare, to regulate persons and property for the welfare of society. By tying conditions to its grants of money to states (conditional "grants-in-aid"), Congress has been able, among other things, to regulate certain aspects of education, secure merit systems in certain branches of the states' civil service, provide old-age assistance, induce the adoption of state unemployment compensation systems, and so on.

Section 8

1. continued: BUT ALL DUTIES, IMPOSTS AND EXCISES SHALL BE UNIFORM THROUGHOUT THE UNITED STATES;

Despite the rule of constitutional interpretation that the Constitution never uses two words when one would do, the words "duty," "impost," and "excise" all overlap more or less. Technically, a "duty" is any monetary obligation to government, whereas an "impost" is a tax on imports or exports; and an "excise" is a "tax imposed on the performance of an act, the engaging in an occupation, or the enjoyment of a privilege"; also on the sale, use or consumption of things, e.g., liquor taxes, tobacco taxes, and taxes on the privilege of using the corporate form for doing business.

The uniformity requirement prevents, for example, the levying of a tax of three cents a pound on tobacco in New York and of four cents a pound in California.

Section 8

2. (In all subsequent paragraphs of Section 8 the words, "The Congress shall have the power" are understood.)

TO BORROW MONEY ON THE CREDIT OF THE UNITED STATES;

Congress borrows money by authorizing the sale of government securities to banks, businesses, and private individuals.

The most important forms of government securities are bonds, treasury certificates, and treasury notes.

Section 8

3. TO REGULATE COMMERCE WITH FOREIGN NATIONS, AND AMONG THE SEVERAL STATES, AND WITH THE INDIAN TRIBES;

The "commerce" clause is another important peg around which Congress has developed a national police power. It is also an excellent demonstration of the fact that the vague words and phrases of certain sections of the Constitution have enabled a document which was written in 1787 in the days of the oxcart to be adapted to the needs of modern industrial society.

"Commerce," in the sense of this clause, includes not only buying and selling (traffic), but all forms of commercial intercourse, of transportation and of communication—even radio broadcasting. Congress' power extends to this commerce if it is carried on with foreign nations, "*affects* more states than one," or is with the Indian tribes. The power of Congress over such commerce is the power to "regulate" it, that is, to *govern* it. In the words of Chief Justice Marshall, this power "is complete in itself, may be exercised to its utmost extent, and acknowledges no limitations other than are prescribed in the Constitution."[10]

Thus Congress is not obliged when regulating "commerce among the states" to consider the effect of its measures on matters which have been generally regulated by the states. Indeed, it may regulate intrastate activities (those within a single state) when these substantially affect interstate or foreign commerce. And while its measures are usually intended to benefit commerce, they are not required to do so. Congress may even prohibit or greatly restrict commerce in order to promote the national health, safety, and welfare, and for humanitarian purposes. Thus in 1807 it proscribed the African slave trade. Many years later it prohibited the transportation of lottery tickets between the states, and, later still, the transportation of liquor into states having "dry laws." Within recent years it has made it a federal crime to use the channels of interstate commerce for the shipping of stolen automobiles, traffic in white slavery, the shipping of impure foods; and has closed the channels of interstate commerce to goods produced under conditions which Congress has defined as "substandard," that is, as detrimental to the health and well-being of the workers. And to make this law effective, Congress has not only banned the interstate transportation of goods so produced, but also has made it a federal offense to *produce* goods under such conditions when the goods are "intended" for sale in interstate commerce (Fair Labor Standards Act). Also, on the other hand, in order to safeguard interstate commerce from interruption by strikes, Congress may regulate employer-employee relations in business and industries which "affect" such commerce, and has done so (the Wagner and Taft-Hartley Acts).[11]

It is also from the "commerce" clause that Congress derives its full powers over the "navigable waters of the United States," including those that may be made navigable by "reasonable improvements." These waters, the Supreme Court has said, "are subject to national planning and control" and the authority of Congress over them "is as broad as the needs of commerce." "Flood protection, watershed development, recovery of the cost of improvements through utilization of power are . . . parts of commerce control."[12]

The "commerce" clause is important, however, not only as a *grant* of power to Congress, but also as a *restriction* on state power. For in giving this power to the national government the Constitution took it away from the states, at least in large part. So whenever a state passes a law, although in professed exercise of its taxing power or police power, and the law materially affects interstate or foreign commerce, the question necessarily arises whether it is not really a regulation of foreign or interstate commerce. And this question is one for the Supreme Court to determine. This branch of its reviewing power is, in fact, one of the two chief fields of the Court's power, the other being that which results from its present-day interpretation of the "due process of law" clause of Amendment XIV (see page 97).

In the exercise of this very great power the Court has first and last handed down hundreds of decisions, some of which involved vast commercial or financial interests; and has laid down scores of rules, about which many voluminous treatises have been written. There is, naturally, no space for such matters in a small book like this. However, the general nature of the Court's task can be briefly stated. It is to weigh the *local* interest against the *general* commercial interest and then to give the right of way to the interest which the Court deems, all things considered, to be the more important one.

But, of course, conditions change and judges change; consequently the Court's judgment of such matters has changed from time to time. Thus the Court's work in this field should be thought of as that of a board of *arbitration* rather than that of a strictly *judicial* body bent on following its own precedents. An illustration or two may be given. About fifty years ago the Court upheld an act of Georgia which forbade the running of freight trains on Sunday—even through trains.[13] Recently, however, it upset an Arizona statute which limited freight trains, including through trains, to seventy cars.[14] Again, in the years preceding the collapse of 1929, the Court was very suspicious of state or local laws which were framed to obtain revenue at the expense of interstate business. But after the collapse, when a majority of the states were on the verge of bankruptcy, it relaxed its standards in such cases very considerably. Nowadays it tends to return to its stricter standards.

There is certainly no field in which the Court's reviewing power has been more valuable than in this. For while we have forty-eight state legislatures, we have *one* national economic and industrial system—*one* prosperity. Nor is there any field in which it has on the whole done better work in maintaining the national authority "in full scope without unnecessary loss of local efficiency."[15] In interpreting the "due process" clause of the Fourteenth Amendment the Court has frequently been lured into questionable positions by that "will-o'-the-wisp" word "liberty"; but "commerce" clause cases are generally down-to-earth cases, well seasoned with facts and figures.[16]

Section 8

4. TO ESTABLISH AN UNIFORM RULE OF NATURALIZATION, AND UNIFORM LAWS ON THE SUBJECT OF BANKRUPTCIES THROUGHOUT THE UNITED STATES;

"Naturalization" is the legal process by which a foreigner is admitted to citizenship.[17] In view of the inherent power of any sovereign nation to determine its own membership, the "naturalization" clause must today be reckoned superfluous. By virtue of this same inherent power, moreover, Congress has the right to say what foreigners may enter the United States or its possessions, for what purposes, and on what conditions; and also to provide for the removal by administrative action of any foreigners who are in the country contrary to the laws.[18]

The main purpose of laws on the subject of "bankruptcies" is to enable debtors to obtain release from their obligations upon the surrender of their property to their creditors. Thus are "the wholly broke made whole again." Congress has passed several such laws, each successive one marking a wider application of the idea.[19]

Section 8

5. TO COIN MONEY, REGULATE THE VALUE THEREOF, AND OF FOREIGN COIN, AND FIX THE STANDARD OF WEIGHTS AND MEASURES;

This power, in conjunction with the power to borrow money on the credit of the United States, gives Congress the authority to issue paper money and make it legal tender for the payment of all debts.

Section 8

6. TO PROVIDE FOR THE PUNISHMENT OF COUNTERFEITING THE SECURITIES AND CURRENT COIN OF THE UNITED STATES;

Congress would have this power even without this clause (see paragraph 18, pages 32–33).

Section 8

7. TO ESTABLISH POST OFFICES AND POST ROADS;

This clause, combined with the power to regulate interstate commerce and to spend for the general welfare, permits Congress to subsidize airlines, railroads, and shipping companies, and to grant money to the states for road building and maintenance. It should be noted, however, that through its powers to tax and spend for the general welfare, Congress could perform these functions even in the absence of this grant. In short, this too is a superfluous clause.

Section 8

8. TO PROMOTE THE PROGRESS OF SCIENCE AND USEFUL ARTS, BY SECURING FOR LIMITED TIMES TO AUTHORS AND INVENTORS THE EXCLUSIVE RIGHT TO THEIR RESPECTIVE WRITINGS AND DISCOVERIES;

Congress has secured to authors, musicians, and artists the protection of copyrights, and to inventors the protection of patents. Anyone who creates by his own skill, labor, and judgment an original book, periodical, lecture, play, musical composition, map, print, photograph, motion picture, or work of art, may secure a copyright by sending two complete copies to the Copyright Office in the Library of Congress and by paying a small fee—in most cases two dollars. The copyright gives to the author an exclusive right to his work for twenty-eight years, and may be renewed once for another twenty-eight years. It may also, like any other property right, be sold, assigned, licensed, or willed.

Persons who invent or discover any *new* and *useful* art, machine, manufacture, composition of matter, certain types of plants, etc., may secure a patent from the Patent Office located in the Department of Commerce. A patent gives the patent holder the exclusive right to his invention or discovery for seventeen years and, like a copyright, may be sold, assigned, or willed. Litigation growing out of conflicting patents may be appealed to a special court—the Court of Customs and Patent Appeals in Washington, D.C.

Congress does not, under this clause, have power to protect trade-marks, which are words, letters, or symbols used in connection with merchandise to point out the ownership and origin of the product, but does have power under the "commerce" clause to protect trade-marks used in interstate commerce. Trade-marks which are registered with the Patent Office need not be original, but merely distinctive. Registration of a trade-mark grants the right to its exclusive use in interstate commerce for twenty years with unlimited rights of renewal.

Section 8

> 9. TO CONSTITUTE TRIBUNALS INFERIOR TO THE SUPREME COURT;

All federal courts except the Supreme Court rest on acts of Congress, and any except the Supreme Court can be abolished by act of Congress.

Section 8

> 10. TO DEFINE AND PUNISH PIRACIES AND FELONIES COMMITTED ON THE HIGH SEAS, AND OFFENSES AGAINST THE LAW OF NATIONS;

Congress can make any crime under international law a crime under national law. In the past this has not been important, because international law has dealt chiefly with *governments* rather than *individuals*. Recent developments placing *individuals* under the obligations of international law may give this paragraph unexpected importance.

Section 8

11. TO DECLARE WAR, GRANT LETTERS OF MARQUE AND
REPRISAL, AND MAKE RULES CONCERNING CAPTURES
ON LAND AND WATER;

The purpose of this clause was to transfer to Congress a power which in Great Britain belonged to the king, that is, to the executive branch. This purpose has not been realized. Especially because of his initiative in the direction of our foreign relations, the President has been primarily responsible for our participation in all of our great wars, and the part of Congress has been that of a rubber stamp.

Letters of marque and reprisal formerly authorized private individuals to prey upon the shipping and property of enemy nations without being considered pirates. Today the Pact of Paris of 1856 bans them.

Section 8

12. TO RAISE AND SUPPORT ARMIES,

Under conditions of total war this and the ensuing clause, plus the inherent powers of the national government in the field of foreign relations (see page 3), confer greater powers than the entire remainder of the Constitution. These include the power to draft men and materials for the armed forces, to establish price ceilings, to requisition property, to allocate and ration materials, to direct the production, marketing, and consumption of all products, and to do whatever is "necessary and proper" to further the successful prosecution of a war. In the words of the late Chief Justice Hughes, "The power to wage war is the power to wage war successfully."[20] It takes real imagination to comprehend the full scope of these powers. Thus it was under these powers that Congress in 1946 established the Atomic Energy Commission and gave it exclusive control of materials, plants, and information dealing with atomic energy—a statute which has been termed "the most remarkable exercise of governmental power" in the entire history of the country.

Section 8

> 12. continued: BUT NO APPROPRIATION OF MONEY TO
> THAT USE [raise and support armies] SHALL BE FOR
> A LONGER TERM THAN TWO YEARS;

This limitation is to ensure the dependence of the Army on Congress and is a reflection of the framers' belief in civilian supremacy and their fear of standing armies. Even this provision (and see page 47) did not assuage the fears of many who, like Thomas Jefferson, felt that standing armies were incompatible with free government. The framers, however, wisely refrained from prohibiting the national government from maintaining an army, but the democratic principle of civilian supremacy still retains its validity. It is illustrated, for example, by the fact that the President, a civilian elective official, is Commander-in-Chief of the Army, Navy, and Air Force.

Section 8

> 13. TO PROVIDE AND MAINTAIN A NAVY;

The Navy was not thought to be a threat to liberty, and no limitations were placed on appropriations for it. Then, too, a two-year limitation would not be feasible, as the construction of naval vessels often takes longer and appropriations have to be pledged in advance.

Inasmuch as the framers did not foresee the development of air power, the recent act of Congress creating the Air Force as an independent element of national military power rests on the general *inherent* power of the national government in the field of foreign relations and national defense (see page 3).

Section 8

> 14. TO MAKE RULES FOR THE GOVERNMENT AND REGULA-
> TION OF THE LAND AND NAVAL FORCES;

The power here conferred is in wartime shared by the President in his capacity as Commander-in-Chief.

15. TO PROVIDE FOR CALLING FORTH THE MILITIA TO EXECUTE THE LAWS OF THE UNION, SUPPRESS INSURRECTIONS AND REPEL INVASIONS;

From an early date the President has been authorized by Congress to employ not only the state militias, but also the Army and Navy against "combinations of persons too powerful to be dealt with" by the ordinary judicial processes. In the exercise of these powers the President may in case of "necessity" declare "martial law." Of this there are various degrees and kinds, the most extreme being that in which military courts temporarily take over the government of a region.[21]

16. TO PROVIDE FOR ORGANIZING, ARMING, AND DISCIPLINING THE MILITIA, AND FOR GOVERNING SUCH PART OF THEM AS MAY BE EMPLOYED IN THE SERVICE OF THE UNITED STATES, RESERVING TO THE STATES RESPECTIVELY, THE APPOINTMENT OF THE OFFICERS, AND THE AUTHORITY OF TRAINING THE MILITIA ACCORDING TO THE DISCIPLINE PRESCRIBED BY CONGRESS;

The states and Congress cooperate in the maintenance of the militia, known today as the National Guard. Normally it operates under the direction of the states, subject to provisions made by Congress. When called into the service of the United States, the National Guard becomes a part of the Army and subject to government by Congress and the President. When not in federal service Congress exercises a considerable degree of control through conditions attached to grants of money to the states for the National Guard.

Section 8

17. TO EXERCISE EXCLUSIVE LEGISLATION IN ALL CASES WHATSOEVER, OVER SUCH DISTRICT (NOT EXCEEDING

TEN MILES SQUARE) AS MAY, BY CESSION OF PARTICU-
LAR STATES, AND THE ACCEPTANCE OF CONGRESS, BE-
COME THE SEAT OF THE GOVERNMENT OF THE UNITED
STATES, AND TO EXERCISE LIKE AUTHORITY OVER ALL
PLACES PURCHASED BY THE CONSENT OF THE LEGIS-
LATURE OF THE STATE IN WHICH THE SAME SHALL
BE, FOR THE ERECTION OF FORTS, MAGAZINES, ARSEN-
ALS, DOCK-YARDS, AND OTHER NEEDFUL BUILDINGS;—
AND

The Constitution does not permit Congress to grant the citizens of the District of Columbia the right to vote in federal elections, but there is no constitutional reason why they should not be allowed to elect their own local officials. At the present time Congress, which has complete governmental powers over the District, spends a day every fortnight it is in session passing city ordinances and serving as city council. The laws are administered by three commissioners (two of whom must be residents of the District, while the third must be a United States Army engineer) appointed by the President with the consent of the Senate. From the point of view of both legislative efficiency and justice for the citizens of the District such a system is indefensible, and the demands for a larger measure of home rule are becoming ever more insistent.

Section 8

18. TO MAKE ALL LAWS WHICH SHALL BE NECESSARY AND
PROPER FOR CARRYING INTO EXECUTION THE FOREGO-
ING POWERS, AND ALL OTHER POWERS VESTED BY THIS
CONSTITUTION IN THE GOVERNMENT OF THE UNITED
STATES, OR IN ANY DEPARTMENT OR OFFICER
THEREOF.

Like the "general welfare" clause, this clause (variously known as the "necessary and proper clause," "elastic clause," "coefficient clause") is subject to misunderstanding. Congress is not here granted the power to make all laws which shall be necessary and proper for any purpose whatsoever, but only to make laws which shall be necessary and proper *in order to execute its enumerated powers or to execute powers vested by the Constitution in the President, the Senate, or the courts.*

In the famous case of McCulloch versus Maryland, Chief Justice Marshall construed the word "necessary" to mean convenient or useful, and rejected the narrow interpretation, "indispensable." He wrote: "Let the end be legitimate, let it be within the scope of the Constitution, and all means which are appropriate, which are plainly adapted to that end, which are not prohibited, but consist with the letter and spirit of the Constitution, are constitutional."[22] As an example: the authority to establish a Federal Reserve Banking System is not among the enumerated powers of Congress, but Congress can do so because it is a "necessary and proper," i.e., *convenient*, way of executing its powers to lay and collect taxes, to borrow money on the credit of the United States, and to regulate interstate commerce.

Section 9

1. THE MIGRATION OR IMPORTATION OF SUCH PERSONS AS ANY OF THE STATES NOW EXISTING SHALL THINK PROPER TO ADMIT, SHALL NOT BE PROHIBITED BY THE CONGRESS PRIOR TO THE YEAR ONE THOUSAND EIGHT HUNDRED AND EIGHT, BUT A TAX OR DUTY MAY BE IMPOSED ON SUCH IMPORTATION, NOT EXCEEDING TEN DOLLARS FOR EACH PERSON.

This paragraph refers to the African slave trade and is of historical interest only.

Section 9

2. THE PRIVILEGE OF THE WRIT OF HABEAS CORPUS SHALL NOT BE SUSPENDED, UNLESS WHEN IN CASES OF REBELLION OR INVASION THE PUBLIC SAFETY MAY REQUIRE IT.

One example of the writ of habeas corpus is an order issued by a court to an arresting officer requiring the latter to bring a specified person before the court and state why he is being held in custody. If the arresting officer cannot justify the holding of the prisoner, the judge will order his release.

Although there is some doubt, it is now generally held that Congress is ordinarily the proper authority to order the suspension of the privilege of the writ in times of rebellion or invasion, subject to review by the courts. But in situations in which the President can validly declare martial law, he can also suspend the writ. The greater power includes the lesser (see page 31).

Section 9

3. NO BILL OF ATTAINDER OR EX POST FACTO LAW SHALL BE PASSED.

A bill of attainder is a legislative conviction and punishment. If Congress should declare that John Doe is a seditionist and order a United States marshal to arrest and imprison him, that would be a bill of attainder, and through a writ of habeas corpus Doe could secure his release. In 1946 the Supreme Court held that this prohibition of bills of attainder invalidated that portion of a congressional appropriation law which declared that three named employees of the Interior Department should be dismissed from government service and disqualified from receiving any compensation from the federal Treasury other than for military or jury service.[23]

An ex post facto law is a retroactive *criminal* law which works to the detriment of any individual, like a law making a particular act a crime which was not a crime when committed, or a law increasing the punishment for a crime after it was committed. The prohibition of ex post facto laws does not prevent the passage of retroactive civil laws or their application retroactively nor to retroactive penal laws which work to the benefit of an accused (for example, a law decreasing a punishment).

· 34 ·

Section 9

> 4. NO CAPITATION, OR OTHER DIRECT TAX SHALL BE LAID, UNLESS IN PROPORTION TO THE CENSUS OR ENUMERATION HEREIN BEFORE DIRECTED TO BE TAKEN.

A capitation tax is a poll or head tax. The precise meaning of the term "direct tax" is today uncertain (see page 127); but no such tax is likely ever again to be attempted.

Section 9

> 5. NO TAX OR DUTY SHALL BE LAID ON ARTICLES EXPORTED FROM ANY STATE.

Although Congress cannot tax articles exported from states, it can, under its power to regulate commerce with foreign nations, prohibit such exports, as by embargoes.

Section 9

> 6. NO PREFERENCE SHALL BE GIVEN BY ANY REGULATION OF COMMERCE OR REVENUE TO THE PORTS OF ONE STATE OVER THOSE OF ANOTHER; NOR SHALL VESSELS BOUND TO, OR FROM, ONE STATE, BE OBLIGED TO ENTER, CLEAR, OR PAY DUTIES IN ANOTHER.

By giving to Congress the power to regulate interstate and foreign commerce, the states were prevented from discriminating against the commerce of their sister states (see page 24). This section prevents Congress in regulating such commerce from discriminating against the trade of any one state or group of states.

Section 9

> 7. NO MONEY SHALL BE DRAWN FROM THE TREASURY, BUT IN CONSEQUENCE OF APPROPRIATIONS MADE BY LAW; AND A REGULAR STATEMENT AND ACCOUNT OF

THE RECEIPTS AND EXPENDITURES OF ALL PUBLIC
MONEY SHALL BE PUBLISHED FROM TIME TO TIME.

It is this clause which, more than any other, gives Congress control over the acts of the other branches of government, the President, the courts, the military, etc., since all depend on Congress for money to carry out their functions.

Section 9

8. NO TITLE OF NOBILITY SHALL BE GRANTED BY THE
UNITED STATES: AND NO PERSON HOLDING ANY OFFICE
OF PROFIT OR TRUST UNDER THEM, SHALL, WITHOUT
THE CONSENT OF THE CONGRESS, ACCEPT OF ANY PRES-
ENT, EMOLUMENT, OFFICE, OR TITLE, OF ANY KIND
WHATEVER, FROM ANY KING, PRINCE, OR FOREIGN
STATE.

Acquainted with the history of previous republican governments, and aware of the tendency of foreign sovereigns to bribe and corrupt republican officials, precautions were taken to prevent any foreign state from securing undue influence within the executive agencies of the national government. The ability of foreign governments to corrupt republican officials by indoctrinating them in communistic, fascistic, and other alien philosophies was not foreseen by the framers.

Section 10

1. NO STATE SHALL ENTER INTO ANY TREATY, ALLIANCE,
OR CONFEDERATION: GRANT LETTERS OF MARQUE AND
REPRISAL;

When the government of the United States was formed, the individual states lost their international personalities, if, in fact, they ever possessed any. Constitutionally the states can neither negotiate with foreign states nor have any direct relations with them. In short, the national government has a complete monopoly over the foreign affairs of the United States.

1. continued: [No state shall] COIN MONEY; EMIT BILLS
OF CREDIT; MAKE ANYTHING BUT GOLD AND SILVER
COIN A TENDER IN PAYMENT OF DEBTS; PASS ANY BILL
OF ATTAINDER, EX POST FACTO LAW, OR LAW IMPAIR-
ING THE OBLIGATION OF CONTRACTS, OR GRANT ANY
TITLE OF NOBILITY.

After the Revolution, the thirteen states, operating under the
weak and ineffective Articles of Confederation, passed through
a difficult period of readjustment as a result of the economic and
political dislocations of the war's aftermath. Many citizens were
in debt, and the farmers who had speculated freely in land while
prices were rising, were especially burdened. Property and
debtor laws were extremely harsh. Debtors were thrown into
jail and deprived of all their holdings. In many states the legislatures, responsive to the pressures of the farmers, passed laws to
alleviate the lot of debtors. Paper money was made legal tender
for the payment of debts, bankruptcy laws were passed, and
sometimes the courts were closed to creditors. These laws, in
turn, aroused the creditor classes, who, feeling that their rights
had been infringed, demanded action to put a stop to such
"abuses" of power by the state legislatures. Creditors, in fact,
were foremost among the groups which brought the Constitutional Convention about, and the prevention of such interferences by the state legislatures with private rights was one
of the major purposes of the Convention. As James Madison put the matter in a speech to his fellow delegates, med-
dlings by the state legislatures with private rights "were evils
which had, more perhaps than anything else, produced this
Convention." Of this feeling the above paragraph was the principal result.

The framers, when they spoke of "contracts" the obligations
of which could not be impaired by state law, had in mind the
ordinary contracts between individuals, especially contracts of
debt. However, the meaning of the word was early expanded by

judicial interpretation to include contracts made by the states themselves, including franchises granted to corporations. As a result the "obligation of contracts" clause became prior to the Civil War the most important defense of the rights of property in the Constitution. States were prevented from passing any law, whether in the interest of the public welfare or not, which might materially disturb rights secured by contract.[24] However, in the late 1830's the Supreme Court began to restrict the application of the "obligation of contracts" clause; and by the 1890's[25] it had been established that all franchises should be narrowly construed in favor of the states and that all contracts impliedly recognized the general police power of the states to regulate property (including contract rights) for the public welfare. Today the "due process" clauses of the Fifth and Fourteenth Amendments have largely replaced the "contract" clause as safeguards of the property right (see page 97).

Section 10

2. NO STATE SHALL, WITHOUT THE CONSENT OF THE CONGRESS, LAY ANY IMPOSTS OR DUTIES ON IMPORTS OR EXPORTS, EXCEPT WHAT MAY BE ABSOLUTELY NECESSARY FOR EXECUTING ITS INSPECTION LAWS: AND THE NET PRODUCE OF ALL DUTIES AND IMPOSTS, LAID BY ANY STATE ON IMPORTS OR EXPORTS, SHALL BE FOR THE USE OF THE TREASURY OF THE UNITED STATES; AND ALL SUCH LAWS SHALL BE SUBJECT TO THE REVISION AND CONTROL OF THE CONGRESS.

Without the express consent of Congress, but subject to congressional revision, states may levy an inspection tax on imports and exports. (Inspection laws are concerned with quantity and quality.) Congress, not the courts, decides whether or not the inspection tax is more than "what may be absolutely necessary for executing . . . inspection laws." With this minor exception, states may not tax imports or exports without the consent of Congress. Imports, goods brought into the country, may not be taxed by a state until they are sold, removed from the original package, or put into the use for which they were imported. Although goods transported from one state to another are not imports, they are protected against arbitrary state taxation by the interstate commerce clause (see page 24).

Section 10

3. NO STATE SHALL, WITHOUT THE CONSENT OF CONGRESS, LAY ANY DUTY OF TONNAGE, KEEP TROOPS, OR SHIPS OF WAR IN TIME OF PEACE, ENTER INTO ANY AGREEMENT OR COMPACT WITH ANOTHER STATE, OR WITH A FOREIGN POWER, OR ENGAGE IN WAR, UNLESS ACTUALLY INVADED, OR IN SUCH IMMINENT DANGER AS WILL NOT ADMIT OF DELAY.

A duty of tonnage is a charge upon a vessel according to its tonnage for entering or leaving a port or navigating on public waters.

A state has the constitutional right without the consent of Congress to provide for and maintain a militia, but it may not keep a standing army.

"Reciprocity statutes" are not compacts. Thus, a Kentucky law granting certain privileges to out-of-state drivers of motor vehicles whose states grant Kentucky drivers the same privileges would not require the consent of Congress; nor would an agreement between neighboring states with respect to tonnage limitations on the public highways. On the other hand, the agreement between New York and New Jersey establishing the New York Port Authority for the governance of the New York harbor rests on congressional approval. It should be added that Congress may give its consent in advance, as it did in 1936 when it authorized any two or more of fourteen named states to enter into compacts for the purpose of controlling the pollution of interstate streams.

Article II—The Executive Article*

Section 1

1. THE EXECUTIVE POWER SHALL BE VESTED IN A PRESI-
DENT OF THE UNITED STATES OF AMERICA.

It is significant that the words "herein granted," which appear in the Legislative Article, are omitted from the Executive Article.* The President has powers other than those which are subsequently enumerated in the remaining clauses of Article II. He has vague and vast "executive powers" which have never been enumerated or defined. In fact, they cannot be defined since their scope depends so largely upon circumstances. Although not so broad, this executive power is akin to the prerogative formerly claimed by the English king to act for the public good "without the prescription of the law, and sometimes even against it . . . "[2] (John Locke). The President can issue proclamations of neutrality, remove executive officials from office, make executive agreements with foreign nations, and take emergency action to preserve the nation (Lincoln), even though such powers are not specifically granted to him by the Constitution.

Section 1

1. continued: HE SHALL HOLD HIS OFFICE DURING THE
TERM OF FOUR YEARS, AND, TOGETHER WITH THE VICE
PRESIDENT, CHOSEN FOR THE SAME TERM, BE ELECTED,
AS FOLLOWS

* Compare this section with Article One, Section 1 which reads: "All legislative powers herein granted shall be vested in a Congress of the United States. . . . "

2. EACH STATE SHALL APPOINT, IN SUCH MANNER AS
THE LEGISLATURE THEREOF MAY DIRECT, A NUMBER
OF ELECTORS, EQUAL TO THE WHOLE NUMBER OF SEN-
ATORS AND REPRESENTATIVES TO WHICH THE STATE
MAY BE ENTITLED IN THE CONGRESS: BUT NO SENA-
TOR OR REPRESENTATIVE, OR PERSON HOLDING AN
OFFICE OF TRUST OR PROFIT UNDER THE UNITED
STATES, SHALL BE APPOINTED AN ELECTOR.

Constitutionally, presidential electors may be chosen in any manner which the legislature of a state may choose. At various times they have been selected by the legislatures themselves, by the voters in districts, by the voters of the entire state, and by a combination of these methods. At the present time, all electors in all states are elected by the voters on a state-wide ticket.

Section 1

3. (This paragraph has been superseded in its en-
tirety by the Twelfth Amendment) THE ELECTORS
SHALL MEET IN THEIR RESPECTIVE STATES, AND VOTE
BY BALLOT FOR TWO PERSONS, OF WHOM ONE AT LEAST
SHALL NOT BE AN INHABITANT OF THE SAME STATE
WITH THEMSELVES. AND THEY SHALL MAKE A LIST
OF ALL THE PERSONS VOTED FOR, AND OF THE NUMBER
OF VOTES FOR EACH; WHICH LIST THEY SHALL SIGN
AND CERTIFY, AND TRANSMIT SEALED TO THE SEAT OF
THE GOVERNMENT OF THE UNITED STATES, DIRECTED
TO THE PRESIDENT OF THE SENATE. THE PRESIDENT
OF THE SENATE SHALL, IN THE PRESENCE OF THE
SENATE AND HOUSE OF REPRESENTATIVES, OPEN ALL
THE CERTIFICATES, AND THE VOTES SHALL THEN BE
COUNTED. THE PERSON HAVING THE GREATEST NUM-
BER OF VOTES SHALL BE THE PRESIDENT, IF SUCH
NUMBER BE A MAJORITY OF THE WHOLE NUM-
BER OF ELECTORS APPOINTED; AND IF THERE BE MORE
THAN ONE WHO HAVE SUCH MAJORITY, AND HAVE
AN EQUAL NUMBER OF VOTES, THEN THE HOUSE

OF REPRESENTATIVES SHALL IMMEDIATELY CHOOSE BY BALLOT ONE OF THEM FOR PRESIDENT; AND IF NO PERSON HAVE A MAJORITY, THEN FROM THE FIVE HIGHEST ON THE LIST THE SAID HOUSE SHALL IN LIKE MANNER CHOOSE THE PRESIDENT. BUT IN CHOOSING THE PRESIDENT, THE VOTES SHALL BE TAKEN BY STATES, THE REPRESENTATION FROM EACH STATE HAVING ONE VOTE; A QUORUM FOR THIS PURPOSE SHALL CONSIST OF A MEMBER OR MEMBERS FROM TWO THIRDS OF THE STATES, AND A MAJORITY OF ALL THE STATES SHALL BE NECESSARY TO A CHOICE. IN EVERY CASE, AFTER THE CHOICE OF THE PRESIDENT, THE PERSON HAVING THE GREATEST NUMBER OF VOTES OF THE ELECTORS SHALL BE THE VICE PRESIDENT. BUT IF THERE SHOULD REMAIN TWO OR MORE WHO HAVE EQUAL VOTES, THE SENATE SHALL CHOOSE FROM THEM BY BALLOT THE VICE PRESIDENT.

The framers had a great deal of difficulty in working out the procedures for selecting the President and Vice-President. Selection by Congress was rejected on the theory that it would make the President dependent on Congress and violate the doctrine of separation of powers. Election by the state legislatures was rejected because of lack of confidence in these bodies which "had betrayed a strong propensity to a variety of pernicious measures."[3] Direct popular election was rejected because the less densely populated states felt that the more populous states would always elect the President, and because most of the delegates were of the opinion that the extent of the country rendered "it impossible that the people can have the requisite capacity to judge of the respective pretensions of the Candidates."[4] So, for lack of something better, they devised the system set forth in Section 1 (3), which they expected would work in somewhat the following fashion: The several state legislatures would prescribe procedures to select the most eminent persons in the states —electors—who would then cast their electoral ballots for the two men they considered the most qualified to serve as President. When the votes of the electors of the various states were collected, the person with the most votes, provided it was a majority of the whole number of electors, was to be declared President; the person with the second highest vote was to be Vice-President. It was expected that almost every elector would cast one vote for an inhabitant of his own state, and the votes would be so dispersed that often no person would have a majority. In this case the House of Representatives, voting by states, would make the final selection from among the five receiving the highest electoral vote.

But the framers reckoned without political parties which, by completely changing the operation of the electoral system, made the original provision for it unworkable. This happened when in the election of 1800 Jefferson and Burr tied in "the Electoral College" for first place. It was the first major breakdown of the constitutional system, and the Twelfth Amendment was needed to repair the breach (see page 108).

Section 1

4. THE CONGRESS MAY DETERMINE THE TIME OF CHOOS-ING THE ELECTORS, AND THE DAY ON WHICH THEY SHALL GIVE THEIR VOTES; WHICH DAY SHALL BE THE SAME THROUGHOUT THE UNITED STATES.

Congress early designated the first Tuesday after the first Monday in November in presidential election years as the day for the selection of electors. Since electors are now ordinarily pledged to cast their ballots for the candidates of their party (see page 110), the November election in effect determines who will be the next President and Vice-President. However, the electors do not give their votes until the first Monday after the second Wednesday in December. On that date the electors assemble at such place as their respective state legislatures direct (normally the state capitol), give their votes and certify six lists, one of which is sent by registered mail to the President of the Senate, two of which are delivered to the Secretary of State of their respective states, two of which are sent by registered mail to the Secretary of State of the United States, and one of which is delivered to the federal district judge of the district in which the electors have assembled. No chances are taken of losing these precious documents, which usually record a foregone certainty. Then on January 6 (see Twentieth Amendment, page 134) the President of the Senate, in the presence of the Senate and the House of Representatives (see Twelfth Amendment, page 108) opens the certificates and the electoral vote is "counted," and the winners are formally proclaimed "elected."[5]

Section 1

5. NO PERSON EXCEPT A NATURAL BORN CITIZEN, OR A CITIZEN OF THE UNITED STATES, AT THE TIME OF THE ADOPTION OF THIS CONSTITUTION, SHALL BE ELIGIBLE TO THE OFFICE OF PRESIDENT;

This clause contains the only constitutional distinction between naturalized and natural-born citizens. Whether a person born abroad of American parents is a natural-born citizen within the meaning of this section has not yet been decided.

Section 1

5. continued: NEITHER SHALL ANY PERSON BE ELIGIBLE TO THAT OFFICE WHO SHALL NOT HAVE ATTAINED TO THE AGE OF THIRTY FIVE YEARS, AND BEEN FOURTEEN YEARS A RESIDENT WITHIN THE UNITED STATES.

The Twelfth Amendment states explicitly that the same qualifications are required for eligibility to the vice-presidency.

Before the election of President Hoover there was some question as to whether the fourteen years' residence requirement meant any fourteen years or fourteen continuous years immediately prior to election. Although a legal resident, Mr. Hoover had been abroad a good part of the fourteen years immediately preceding his election. His election settled any doubts, and the interpretation of this requirement came from the most authentic source—the same source which created the Constitution—the people.

Section 1

6. IN CASE OF THE REMOVAL OF THE PRESIDENT FROM OFFICE, OR OF HIS DEATH, RESIGNATION, OR INABILITY TO DISCHARGE THE POWERS AND DUTIES OF THE SAID OFFICE, THE SAME SHALL DEVOLVE ON THE VICE PRESIDENT, AND THE CONGRESS MAY BY LAW PROVIDE FOR THE CASE OF REMOVAL, DEATH, RESIGNATION OR INABILITY, BOTH OF THE PRESIDENT AND VICE PRESIDENT, DECLARING WHAT OFFICER SHALL THEN ACT AS PRESIDENT, AND SUCH OFFICER SHALL ACT ACCORDINGLY UNTIL, THE DISABILITY BE REMOVED, OR A PRESIDENT SHALL BE ELECTED.

Although the person who assumes office in case of removal, death, etc., of both the President and Vice-President only *acts* as President, the Vice-President becomes President when the President *dies*. John Tyler established this precedent when he succeeded to the presidency on Harrison's death and proceeded to sign all state papers "John Tyler, President of the United States."

The "powers and duties" of the presidency devolve upon the Vice-President in the event of the disability of the President, but Congress has never determined who shall judge whether or not the President is unable to discharge his duties. Twice in our history this question has caused difficulty: when President Garfield suffered a lingering death from an assassin's bullet, and when President Wilson had a physical breakdown during the closing years of his second term. Some provision should be made for procedures to determine what constitutes incapacity, but the details need to be carefully worked out because of the danger of abuse.

If the Vice-President dies or becomes incapacitated, the line of presidential succession under a recent act of Congress is the

Speaker of the House, the President pro tempore of the Senate, the Secretary of State, the Secretary of the Treasury, the Secretary of Defense, the Attorney General, the Postmaster General, the Secretary of Agriculture, the Secretary of the Interior, the Secretary of Commerce, and the Secretary of Labor. But none of these may succeed unless he possesses the constitutional qualifications of a President.[6]

Section 1

7. THE PRESIDENT SHALL, AT STATED TIMES, RECEIVE FOR HIS SERVICES, A COMPENSATION, WHICH SHALL NEITHER BE INCREASED NOR DIMINISHED DURING THE PERIOD FOR WHICH HE SHALL HAVE BEEN ELECTED,[*]

To preserve the President's independence, Congress is prohibited from diminishing his salary during the period for which he is elected. Its increase is also prohibited because the framers feared that it might be used as a bargaining weapon.

Section 1

7. continued: AND HE SHALL NOT RECEIVE WITHIN THAT PERIOD ANY OTHER EMOLUMENT FROM THE UNITED STATES, OR ANY OF THEM.

This provision was inserted to prevent the President's own state from compensating him and to ensure his independence from any state. He is totally dependent upon the federal government for his salary, which is now $100,000 per year. He also receives free the use of the White House, secretarial and executive assistance, and $40,000 annually for traveling expenses plus $50,000 annually for general purposes.

Section 1

8. BEFORE HE ENTER ON THE EXECUTION OF HIS OFFICE, HE SHALL TAKE THE FOLLOWING OATH OR AFFIRMA-

[*] This accounts for the rush to push through Congress a bill increasing President Truman's salary before his new term began on January 20.

TION:—"I DO SOLEMNLY SWEAR (OR AFFIRM) THAT I WILL FAITHFULLY EXECUTE THE OFFICE OF PRESIDENT OF THE UNITED STATES, AND WILL TO THE BEST OF MY ABILITY, PRESERVE, PROTECT AND DEFEND THE CONSTITUTION OF THE UNITED STATES."

The Chief Justice of the Supreme Court normally administers this oath or affirmation, but any judicial officer may do so. Calvin Coolidge's father, a justice of the peace, administered the oath to his son.

Section 2

1. THE PRESIDENT SHALL BE COMMANDER IN CHIEF OF THE ARMY AND NAVY OF THE UNITED STATES, AND OF THE MILITIA OF THE SEVERAL STATES, WHEN CALLED INTO THE ACTUAL SERVICE OF THE UNITED STATES;

A civilian, the President, is Commander-in-Chief of our armed forces. This is another provision to ensure civilian supremacy over the military. The Constitution does not forbid the President to assume active command of troops in the field, but no President has ever done so.

Congress shares with the President his authority over the armed forces. It supplies the money and makes regulations for their governance. It has the power to "declare war"; but the President is able to give orders to the Army, Navy, and Air Force that may lead to hostilities, as well as to direct our foreign relations to that end. Thus President Polk, by sending troops into disputed territory, deliberately precipitated the Mexican War. An example of the President's power over the armed forces which had amusing rather than serious consequences occurred when President Theodore Roosevelt sent the Navy halfway around the world after Congress had threatened to withhold appropriations for a global tour. Congress was then presented with the unreal choice of appropriating money to bring the fleet home or leaving it where it was.

The President appoints all military officers with the consent of the Senate. He governs hostile territories subjugated by our Armed Forces until their disposition is determined by Congress or by treaty. And as Commander-in-Chief he has within his hands the ultimate decision of all matters of strategy.

But his powers are vastly more than purely military ones. During the Civil War, President Lincoln, as "a war measure" and without congressional authorization, declared all slaves in areas in rebellion to be "free." (Proclamation of Emancipation.) Moreover, the President's powers as Commander-in-Chief are augmented by his "executive powers," and by such powers as Congress may delegate to him (see page 2). Under the conditions of total war, when the distinction between soldier and civilian is blurred and when the entire Nation is in arms the resulting "aggregate of powers" is very great. Nevertheless, it is not unlimited; and outside the "theater of war" the courts will review his acts. For example, during the Second World War President Roosevelt authorized the Army to create "defense zones" on the West Coast, and under his order (supported by an act of Congress), 112,000 Japanese, of whom two-thirds were citizens of the United States, were forced out of their homes and put in concentration camps. These measures were reviewed and sustained by the Supreme Court on the general ground of military necessity.[7] On the other hand, the President's order establishing martial law in Hawaii after Pearl Harbor was held by the Court to have lacked such justification and, therefore, to have been unconstitutional.[8]

Section 2

1. continued: HE [the President] MAY REQUIRE THE OPINION, IN WRITING, OF THE PRINCIPAL OFFICER IN EACH OF THE EXECUTIVE DEPARTMENTS, UPON ANY SUBJECT RELATING TO THE DUTIES OF THEIR RESPECTIVE OFFICES,

Although there is no mention of the Cabinet in the Constitution, that body came into existence as early as 1793 and from the beginning the President's power over the heads of the major executive departments has extended beyond merely requiring written reports upon subjects relating to the duties of their respective offices. These officers serve at the President's pleasure, and his control over their official acts is complete. On the other hand, the executive departments, and usually their duties, are created by law, and the money needed for their operation comes from Congress.

Section 2

1. continued: AND HE SHALL HAVE POWER TO GRANT REPRIEVES AND PARDONS FOR OFFENSES *against the United States* EXCEPT IN CASES OF IMPEACHMENT.

A reprieve postpones punishment. A full pardon restores a man to citizenship and restores his legal status in other respects. The President can pardon before or after conviction or during the trial, but cannot pardon before the commission of a crime. He cannot, in other words, exempt anyone from the law.

Section 2

2. HE SHALL HAVE POWER, BY AND WITH THE ADVICE AND CONSENT OF THE SENATE, TO MAKE TREATIES, PROVIDED TWO THIRDS OF THE SENATORS PRESENT CONCUR;

Although the President, through the Secretary of State, is free to seek the advice of senatorial leaders, especially members of the Senate Committee on Foreign Relations, the Senate has usually done very little advising. The President negotiates the treaty, and then presents it to the Senate for its approval. Prior to 1929 Senate consideration of treaties took place in "executive session," behind closed doors, unless the Senate specially ordered otherwise. The final step in the making of a treaty is its ratification, which is the President's act.

There are several explanations of the two-thirds vote requirement. The Southern states were afraid that their Northern sisters—who were in a majority—would negotiate trade conventions which would be disadvantageous to the South. They remembered that John Jay of New York, Secretary of Foreign Affairs under the Confederation, had proposed a treaty with Spain conceding the right to close the mouth of the Mississippi at New Orleans in return for concessions to Northern merchants. The two-thirds rule gives sectional groups a veto upon such treaties. In addition, moreover, to being international compacts, treaties are "supreme law of the land," so that their provisions are often enforced by courts just like any other law, and this fact too is sometimes urged in favor of the two-thirds requirement.

Nevertheless, now that the United States is a world leader and takes a continuous part in international negotiations, the two-thirds rule has conspicuous disadvantages. For political and other reasons it is often extremely difficult to secure the consent of two thirds of the senators on any measure. The two-thirds rule permits only one more than one third of the senators, representing perhaps a minority of the population, to block treaties desired by the majority. Many have suggested that ratification be by a simple majority of *both* houses of Congress; and unquestionably it would be more realistic to include the House of Representatives in the ratification procedure, since that body has to approve any appropriations and legislation that may be necessary to carry out the terms of a treaty.

Not surprisingly, various ways have been devised from time to time to get around the difficulties imposed by the treaty-making process. One is the joint resolution of Congress—an ordinary legislative procedure. Texas was annexed in this fashion after the Senate refused to do so by treaty. Another device is the executive agreement, of which there are two types: (1) In the field of foreign affairs Congress and the President have cognate powers, and it is constitutionally permissible for Congress to delegate to the President larger powers than would be allowable in domestic affairs. Thus, the President is often empowered by Congress to make executive agreements, e.g., reciprocal tariff agreements. (2) As part of his undefined executive powers, growing out of his power to appoint and receive diplomatic officials, and as the nation's official spokesman, the President has the power to negotiate agreements with foreign nations which do not require the consent of Congress. As long as these agreements are not countermanded by Congress they, like treaties, become "law of the land." It was once thought that executive agreements differed from treaties in that they were concerned with affairs of less importance. But in fact executive agreements have sometimes dealt with highly important matters, e.g., in September, 1940, President Roosevelt handed over to Great Britain fifty naval vessels in exchange for certain leases of military bases. Apparently the only certain distinction between a treaty and an executive agreement today is that a treaty requires confirmation by "two thirds of the Senators present," whereas an executive agreement is not submitted to the Senate. Again we see how the Constitution is developed by action under it.[9]

Section 2

2. continued: AND HE [the President] SHALL NOMI-
NATE, AND BY AND WITH THE ADVICE AND CONSENT
OF THE SENATE, SHALL APPOINT AMBASSADORS, OTHER
PUBLIC MINISTERS AND CONSULS, JUDGES OF THE
SUPREME COURT, AND ALL OTHER OFFICERS OF THE
UNITED STATES, WHOSE APPOINTMENTS ARE NOT
HEREIN OTHERWISE PROVIDED FOR, AND WHICH SHALL
BE ESTABLISHED BY LAW; BUT THE CONGRESS MAY BY
LAW VEST THE APPOINTMENT OF SUCH INFERIOR OF-
FICERS, AS THEY THINK PROPER, IN THE PRESIDENT
ALONE, IN THE COURTS OF LAW, OR IN THE HEADS OF
DEPARTMENTS.

Those officers who are appointed by the President by and with the advice and consent of the Senate (only a majority vote is required) are known as superior or senatorial officers. Officers who can, if Congress permits, be appointed by the President alone, by the courts, or by heads of departments are known as "inferior" officers.

The Senate has normally refused to approve local federal appointments over the objection of the senator from the state in which the office is located, provided the senator is of the same party as the President. This practice, known as "senatorial courtesy," permits the senators to veto presidential appointments, and gives them extensive control over federal patronage in their several states. Because of this custom, senators from the state in which the appointment is to be made are usually consulted by the President before he sends the appointments to the Senate for confirmation.

Section 2

3. THE PRESIDENT SHALL HAVE POWER TO FILL UP ALL VACANCIES THAT MAY HAPPEN DURING THE RECESS OF THE SENATE, BY GRANTING COMMISSIONS WHICH SHALL EXPIRE AT THE END OF THEIR NEXT SESSION.

The word "happen" here has come to mean *happen to exist*. Thus the clause permits the President to fill temporarily *any* vacancies while the Senate is recessed, no matter how or when they occurred.

Section 3

1. HE SHALL FROM TIME TO TIME GIVE TO THE CONGRESS INFORMATION OF THE STATE OF THE UNION, AND RECOMMEND TO THEIR CONSIDERATION SUCH MEASURES AS HE SHALL JUDGE NECESSARY AND EXPEDIENT;

The opening address of the President at each annual session is known as the State of the Union Message. Washington and John Adams gave their addresses in person, but Jefferson sent his in writing. President Wilson revived the practice of personally delivering the speech.

At the beginning of each session the President is also required by law to send to Congress a Budget Message and an Economic Report. From time to time he sends messages, addresses Congress on specific subjects, and makes recommendations for legislation. In this manner he is able to focus national attention on national problems. As an extension of this practice, a great many bills, although formally introduced by congressmen, actually originate in the executive departments.

Section 3

1. continued: HE MAY, ON EXTRAORDINARY OCCASIONS, CONVENE BOTH HOUSES, OR EITHER OF THEM,

Whenever the President thinks it necessary, he can call special sessions of Congress. Once in session, Congress has full powers. In contrast, some of the state legislatures when called into special session are limited to discussion and action on the particular matters laid before them by the Governor.

The Senate has frequently, the House never, been called into special session by itself. The reason for the difference is that the Senate has been summoned to ratify treaties and appointments, which it does without the concurrence of the House.

Section 3

1. continued: AND IN CASE OF DISAGREEMENT BETWEEN THEM, WITH RESPECT TO THE TIME OF ADJOURNMENT, HE MAY ADJOURN THEM TO SUCH TIME AS HE SHALL THINK PROPER;

The President has never been called upon to exercise this duty.

Section 3

1. continued: HE SHALL RECEIVE AMBASSADORS AND OTHER PUBLIC MINISTERS;

The President is the only officer who can speak officially for the United States to foreign countries. Conversely, foreign governments may speak to the United States only through the

President, usually via his agent, the Secretary of State. The President's power to receive ambassadors includes the power to recognize new states or governments.

The nature of the problems of foreign policy requires that the initiative and general direction be in the President's hands. The increasing importance of foreign relations during the last several decades accounts in no small part for the increasing powers of the President in all fields.

Section 3

    1. continued: HE SHALL TAKE CARE THAT THE LAWS BE FAITHFULLY EXECUTED, AND SHALL COMMISSION ALL THE OFFICERS OF THE UNITED STATES.

This clause, plus the undefined "executive power" clause, gives the President unrestricted power to remove all *executive* officers. He is charged with the duty of faithfully executing the laws and therefore must have control over those officers through whom he operates. This removal power, however, does not extend to officers who have "quasi-legislative" or "quasi-judicial" functions conferred upon them by act of Congress, such as do members of the Federal Trade Commission, Interstate Commerce Commission, or the Atomic Energy Commission. Such officers may be removed only in accordance with law.[10]

As was pointed out on a previous page (see page 31), Congress very early authorized the President to use the armed forces when necessary to overcome combinations too powerful to be dealt with by the courts in the enforcement of the laws. Thus, the President's duty to see that the laws are enforced is supported by his powers as Commander-in-Chief.

Section 4

    1. THE PRESIDENT, VICE PRESIDENT AND ALL CIVIL OFFICERS OF THE UNITED STATES, SHALL BE REMOVED FROM OFFICE ON IMPEACHMENT FOR, AND CONVIC-

All but military officers of the United States are liable to impeachment. Congressmen are not officers of the United States within the meaning of this section and can be removed from office only by a two-thirds vote of their respective houses.

The punishment for impeachment extends only to removal from office and disqualification from holding any office of profit or trust under the United States, but the impeached officer may be subjected to subsequent criminal proceedings (see page 11).

Jefferson attempted to turn the impeachment procedure into a device for political control. He felt that incompetent or politically objectionable officers, especially judicial officers, who had not committed a legal wrong, should, nevertheless, be liable to impeachment and removal from office. He failed, however, to get this interpretation accepted; unfitness, incompetence, etc., are not grounds for impeachment—the officer must be guilty of a legal wrong or something approaching that.

Article III—The Judicial Article

Section 1

1. THE JUDICIAL POWER OF THE UNITED STATES, SHALL
BE VESTED IN ONE SUPREME COURT, AND IN SUCH
INFERIOR COURTS AS THE CONGRESS MAY FROM TIME
TO TIME ORDAIN AND ESTABLISH.

The Supreme Court is the only federal court that is definitely required by the Constitution. The Founding Fathers were purposely vague as to the nature of the court system because they were unable to agree as to the need for inferior federal courts. Under present legislation there are eighty-four district courts, and ten circuit courts of appeal inferior to the Supreme Court. There are other federal courts (e.g., the district court and circuit court of appeals for the District of Columbia, the Court of Claims, the Customs Court, the Court of Customs and Patent Appeals) which Congress has established under powers granted to it by other sections of the Constitution. Over these so-called "legislative courts" Congress has more control than it has over the regular inferior federal courts.

Although the Constitution vests the judicial power of the United States in the Supreme and inferior courts, Congress determines to a large extent the distribution of this power among the federal courts.

Judicial power is the power of a court to pronounce a judgment and carry it into effect between persons and parties who bring a case before it for decision.[1] The case must be a real and substantial legal controversy between parties having actual or possible adverse interests. Unlike the International Court of Justice and some state courts, the federal courts refuse to give advisory opinions. They may, however, render "declaratory judgments" on the respective rights of parties in order to head off litigation between them, or to free one or both of them from uncertainty regarding their rights, as, say, under an ambiguous contract; and such judgments are binding on both parties.

Section 1

1. continued: THE JUDGES, BOTH OF THE SUPREME AND INFERIOR COURTS, SHALL HOLD THEIR OFFICES DURING GOOD BEHAVIOR, AND SHALL, AT STATED TIMES, RECEIVE FOR THEIR SERVICES A COMPENSATION, WHICH SHALL NOT BE DIMINISHED DURING THEIR CONTINUANCE IN OFFICE.

The Constitution provides for the appointment of judges by the President with the consent of the Senate (see pages 51–52), but it is silent as to the size of the courts and the qualifications of the judges. Today there are nine members of the Supreme Court, but at various times the number has been six, seven, and ten. The number of judges serving on a district court or a circuit court of appeals varies with the number and nature of the cases to be handled.

Although the Constitution here refers to members of both the Supreme and inferior courts as judges, in Article I, Section 3 (6) it refers to the "Chief Justice" (see page 11), and since the Judiciary Act of 1789 members of the Supreme Court have always been referred to as "Justice"—more formally as "Mr. Justice."

The term "good behavior" means virtually for life, since a federal judge can be removed from office only through the regular impeachment process.

In order to ensure the independence of the judiciary, Congress is prohibited from decreasing a judge's salary during his term in office, although (unlike the President's) it may be increased. The Supreme Court formerly held that income taxes could not be levied against the salaries of federal judges, but this decision was reversed in 1937—judges are protected only from decreases which are specifically directed at their compensation.

Section 2

1. THE JUDICIAL POWER SHALL EXTEND TO ALL CASES, IN LAW AND EQUITY, ARISING UNDER THIS CONSTITUTION, THE LAWS OF THE UNITED STATES, AND TREATIES MADE, OR WHICH SHALL BE MADE, UNDER THEIR AUTHORITY;

This means that the judicial power of the federal courts *may be extended by Congress* to all cases in which it is necessary to interpret the Constitution, or some law or treaty of the United States in order to dispose of the case. Thus if X is tried and convicted under state law in a state court for murder, he can still appeal to the United States Supreme Court to pass on his contention that his trial was not a fair one under the "due process" clause of Amendment XIV (see pages 119–121).

"Cases in law and equity": The distinction is inherited from England. In the former the party bringing the case usually asks for damages; in the latter he usually asks for an injunction. Thus the common law is supposed to compensate for injury already done, while equity tries to prevent the injury from occurring.

Section 2

1. continued: TO ALL CASES AFFECTING AMBASSADORS, OTHER PUBLIC MINISTERS AND CONSULS;

This refers to *foreign* ambassadors, public ministers, and consuls. For the federal courts to assume jurisdiction, these officials must be materially affected by the case without necessarily being parties to it. Since the national government is responsible for good relations between the United States and foreign governments, it was reasoned that cases affecting foreign public ministers should be within the judicial power of the United States.

Section 2

1. continued: TO ALL CASES OF ADMIRALTY AND MARITIME JURISDICTION;

This jurisdiction is concerned with ships and shipping. Under the English rule it extended only to the high seas and those rivers in which the tide ebbed and flowed. Under the Constitution, however, such jurisdiction reaches all "navigable waters of the United States" whether or not subject to the ebb and flow of the tide.

Section 2

1. continued: TO CONTROVERSIES TO WHICH THE UNITED STATES SHALL BE A PARTY; TO CONTROVERSIES BETWEEN TWO OR MORE STATES; BETWEEN A STATE AND CITIZENS OF ANOTHER STATE;

The Eleventh Amendment modified the underlined portion of this section (see page 106).

Section 2

1. continued: BETWEEN CITIZENS OF DIFFERENT STATES,—

These are called "diversity of citizenship cases." Congress has legislated that such cases involving amounts of less than $3,000 shall not be entertained by the federal courts (although they may be brought there for other reasons—e.g., interpretation of a federal law or of the Constitution).

Section 2

1. continued: BETWEEN CITIZENS OF THE SAME STATE CLAIMING LANDS UNDER GRANTS OF DIFFERENT STATES, AND

At the time of the adoption of the Constitution many states had conflicting claims to Western lands. Today this section is unimportant.

Section 2

> 1. continued: BETWEEN A STATE, OR THE CITIZENS
> THEREOF, AND FOREIGN STATES, CITIZENS OR SUBJECTS.

This clause also was modified by the Eleventh Amendment (see page 106).

In summary, the judicial power of the United States extends to the following cases in law and equity:

To certain cases because of the *nature of the dispute:*

> *a.* Cases arising under the Constitution, a federal law, or a federal treaty.
> *b.* Cases arising under admiralty and maritime jurisdiction.
> *c.* Cases involving land title which is claimed because of grants of two or more states.

To certain cases *because of the parties to the dispute:*

> *a.* Cases in which the United States is a party.
> *b.* Cases in which a state is a party.
> *c.* Cases in which the parties are citizens of different states.
> *d.* Cases which affect foreign ambassadors, ministers, and consuls.

With the exception of the original jurisdiction granted to the Supreme Court (see below page 61), Congress determines which, if any, of the federal courts shall exercise the jurisdiction granted by the Constitution.

The mere fact that the Constitution grants power over certain types of cases to the federal courts does not, of itself, exclude state courts from exercising concurrent jurisdiction. But Congress is free to make the federal jurisdiction exclusive and has done so in the following cases: crimes and offenses against the United States; suits for penalties and forfeiture authorized by the laws of the United States; civil cases of admiralty and maritime jurisdiction; prize cases (cases arising out of the capture of enemy or abandoned property on the high seas); cases involving patent and copyright laws of the United States; cases arising under bankruptcy laws of the United States; cases in which a state is a party (except between a state and its citizens or a state and citizens of another state or foreign country); and cases involving ambassadors and other public ministers.

Within any state there are two court systems, the state court system and the federal court system, neither of which is superior or inferior to the other. Over some matters both systems have jurisdiction, over others only the state courts, and for still others only the federal courts have jurisdiction. A dispute between two citizens of New York over the terms of a contract signed in New York would be within the exclusive jurisdiction of the New York courts. A suit involving more than $3,000 between citizens of different states would be within the jurisdiction of both the federal courts and the courts of the state in which the defendant is located. A suit arising under the Sherman Antitrust Law would be within the exclusive jurisdiction of the federal courts.

Section 2

2. IN ALL CASES AFFECTING AMBASSADORS, OTHER PUBLIC MINISTERS AND CONSULS, AND THOSE IN WHICH A STATE SHALL BE PARTY, THE SUPREME COURT SHALL HAVE ORIGINAL JURISDICTION. IN ALL THE OTHER CASES BEFORE MENTIONED, THE SUPREME COURT SHALL HAVE APPELLATE JURISDICTION, BOTH AS TO LAW AND FACT, WITH SUCH EXCEPTIONS, AND UNDER SUCH REGULATIONS AS THE CONGRESS SHALL MAKE.

Original jurisdiction is the power to hear and decide cases in the first instance. Appellate jurisdiction is the power to hear and decide appeals from the decisions of lower courts. In all cases, except those mentioned above, the Supreme Court has only appellate jurisdiction, and furthermore only such appellate jurisdiction as is specifically granted to it by Congress. The completeness of the control by Congress of the Supreme Court's appellate jurisdiction is illustrated by the following: In 1868 the Supreme Court announced that it would hear the appeal of a certain newspaper editor who challenged the constitutionality of one of the Reconstruction Acts. After the Court had heard the case argued and was still considering its decision, Congress passed a law which prevented the appeal of that type of case to the Supreme Court, which thereupon held that it had no power to decide the case. The result was that the Court lost an opportunity to pass upon the constitutionality of the Reconstruction Acts.[2]

Despite the great and increasing volume of federal litigation, the Supreme Court has been able to keep up with its work because Congress has within recent years given it wide authority to select only the most important cases for review. The Supreme Court must, however, review the following types of cases when asked to do so by a disappointed litigant:

A. When the highest state court competent to hear a case in which it is necessary to interpret the Constitution, a federal law, or a federal treaty *rejects* a litigant's interpretation of any of these, the Supreme Court must accept the case. For example, if X, a Negro, is convicted by State Y for murder by a jury from which Negroes were excluded, he could invoke the Fourteenth Amendment (see page 120). If the highest state court competent to review the case rejects X's interpretation of this Amendment, he has a *right* to a review by the Supreme Court.

B. When a federal circuit court of appeals strikes down a state law or action as repugnant to the Constitution, a federal law, or a federal treaty, the Supreme Court must review the case if it is brought before it.

C. When a federal district court holds a federal penal statute unconstitutional, enjoins enforcement of a state or federal statute, or decides a case under the antitrust laws, the disappointed litigant may carry the case directly to the Supreme Court and the Court must review the case.

With the exception of these cases the Supreme Court has discretion as to whether or not it will review a case. It accepts, "on writ of certiorari," only those which it considers to be of sufficient public importance to merit its attention.

Section 2

3. THE TRIAL OF ALL CRIMES, EXCEPT IN CASES OF IM-
PEACHMENT, SHALL BE BY JURY; AND SUCH TRIAL
SHALL BE HELD IN THE STATE WHERE THE SAID CRIMES
SHALL HAVE BEEN COMMITTED; BUT WHEN NOT COM-
MITTED WITHIN ANY STATE, THE TRIAL SHALL BE
AT SUCH PLACE OR PLACES AS THE CONGRESS MAY BY
LAW HAVE DIRECTED.

This section guarantees the right to a trial by jury to persons accused of a crime by the national government. (See also Amendment VI.)

Section 3

1. TREASON AGAINST THE UNITED STATES, SHALL CONSIST
ONLY IN LEVYING WAR AGAINST THEM, OR IN ADHER-
ING TO THEIR ENEMIES, GIVING THEM AID AND COM-
FORT. NO PERSON SHALL BE CONVICTED OF TREASON
UNLESS ON THE TESTIMONY OF TWO WITNESSES TO
THE SAME OVERT ACT, OR ON CONFESSION IN OPEN
COURT.

This section does not prevent Congress from making "sedition" a capital crime, i.e., using force and violence short of war in opposition to the laws, or conspiring to do so. It is possible for an alien to commit treason against the United States because while within the boundaries of the United States he owes our government temporary allegiance.

No person may be convicted of treason on the basis of circumstantial evidence alone. The accused must make a confession in open court, or there must be two witnesses to the overt act, which act, either by itself or *along with other evidence*, convinces the jury of the defendant's guilt.

2. THE CONGRESS SHALL HAVE POWER TO DECLARE THE
PUNISHMENT OF TREASON, BUT NO ATTAINDER OF
TREASON SHALL WORK CORRUPTION OF BLOOD, OR FOR-
FEITURE EXCEPT DURING THE LIFE OF THE PERSON
ATTAINED.

In sixteenth- and seventeenth-century England "attainders of treason" worked "corruption of blood," thereby making it impossible for the traitor's family to inherit from him. Having been traitors themselves in rebelling against King George, the framers may have felt a certain tenderness for such unfortunates.

Judicial Review

Although the Constitution does not specifically grant to the courts the power to nullify legislation which violates their interpretation of the Constitution, it furnishes sufficient verbal basis for the power. For the first assertion of the power—the most unique aspect of our constitutional system—against an act of Congress, we are indebted to Chief Justice John Marshall's famous decision, in 1803, in the great case of Marbury versus Madison. The case, which was preceded by several similar holdings in some of the states under their constitutions, arose out of the following facts:

The Federalist party had lost the election of 1800, but before leaving office they succeeded in creating several new judicial posts. Among these were forty-two justice-of-peaceships for the District of Columbia, to which the retiring Federalist President, John Adams, appointed forty-two Federalists. The Senate confirmed these appointments and the commissions were signed and sealed, but Adams' Secretary of State, John Marshall, failed to deliver certain of them. When the new President, Thomas Jefferson, assumed office, he instructed his Secretary of State, James Madison, not to deliver seventeen of these commissions, including one for William Marbury. Marbury decided to take action, and consulting the law he found that Section 13 of the

Judiciary Act of 1789 declared: "The Supreme Court . . . shall have the power to issue . . . writs of mandamus, in cases warranted by the principles and usages of law, to . . . persons holding office, under the authority of the United States." (A writ of mandamus is a court order directed to an officer requiring him to perform a certain "ministerial" duty as required by law.) Without further ado, Marbury, through his attorneys, went before the Supreme Court and asked the justices to issue a writ of mandamus to Secretary Madison ordering him to deliver the commission. The Court, speaking through Marshall, who had now become Chief Justice, held that Section 13 of the Judiciary Act of 1789 was repugnant to Article III, Section 2 of the Constitution (see page 61) inasmuch as the Constitution itself limited the Supreme Court's "original" jurisdiction to cases affecting public ambassadors or those to which a state was party. Therefore, the Court refused to issue the mandamus.

Whence did the Supreme Court get the authority thus to gainsay Congress? Marshall reasoned that the Constitution is law, that it is the duty of courts to interpret the law in order to decide cases in accordance with it, and that therefore the Supreme Court had the authority and was duty-bound to interpret the Constitution, and of course to prefer it to any other law. He also pointed out that the Constitution enjoins the courts to enforce as the supreme law of the land only those acts of Congress which are "in pursuance of the Constitution" Article VI, (Section 2, see page 79). Hence the Court must first determine whether a law *is* in pursuance of the Constitution before it is entitled to enforce it as "law of the land."

While this argument is logically a very cogent one, there continues to be heated debate to this day concerning the soundness of the result. Thus critics, including several Presidents, have argued that the Constitution is "supreme law" because it emanates from the people, and that therefore the most immediately responsible agencies, Congress and the President, ought to have at least as good right to interpret it as the least politically responsible agency—the Supreme Court.

Also, Marshall's assumption that the Constitution is law in

the ordinary sense and hence suited to judicial interpretation has been questioned. The Constitution, it is argued, is a *political* document and consequently not susceptible to interpretation by the ordinary judicial processes. Nor have critics of judicial review accepted the argument that it is a necessary check on Congress and the President. They argue that Congress and the President are checked by the voters, whereas the only check on the judges is their own self-restraint, which seems at times to be lacking.

Most of the criticism of judicial review is directed, it should be noted, against review of acts of Congress, which is today rarely exercised adversely to such acts. That there must be a central review by the Supreme Court over state action is generally conceded. As Justice Holmes once put the matter: "I do not think the United States would come to an end if we lost our power to declare an Act of Congress void. I do think the Union would be imperiled if we could not make that declaration as to the laws of the several states."[3]

Article IV—Interstate Relations

Section 1

1. FULL FAITH AND CREDIT SHALL BE GIVEN IN EACH
STATE TO THE PUBLIC ACTS, RECORDS, AND JUDICIAL
PROCEEDINGS OF EVERY OTHER STATE. AND THE CON-
GRESS MAY BY GENERAL LAWS PRESCRIBE THE MAN-
NER IN WHICH SUCH ACTS, RECORDS AND PROCEEDINGS
SHALL BE PROVED, AND THE EFFECT THEREOF.

This clause applies especially to judicial decisions. Suppose a
Pennsylvania court awards X a $5,000 judgment against Y, also
a Pennsylvanian; but then, after moving to New York, Y refuses
to pay up. Thanks to the full faith and credit clause, X does not
have to start a new suit against Y in New York. The New York
courts will give full faith and credit to the Pennsylvania judgment and will enforce it just as they would a similar judgment of
the New York courts.

Or suppose that X, a New Yorker, while driving his car in
New Jersey injures Y or his property, and then returns to New
York without doing anything about it. Following a certain procedure, Y may sue X in the New Jersey courts, and if they decide in his favor, the New York courts will be obliged to aid
Y in collecting the judgment in his favor—whether X appeared
in the case or not.

Suppose again that X, a North Carolinian, goes to Nevada
and obtains a divorce after a few weeks' sojourn there—are other
states obliged to honor the divorce? In 1945 the Supreme Court
said, no, because the Nevada court "lacked jurisdiction" of the

case, X not being a bona fide resident of the state.[1] But in June, 1948, this decision was practically canceled by another which says that state courts are final judges of their own jurisdiction in such cases. Thus was the green light given to easy divorce.[2]

Section 2

1. continued: THE CITIZENS OF EACH STATE SHALL BE ENTITLED TO ALL PRIVILEGES AND IMMUNITIES OF CITIZENS IN THE SEVERAL STATES.

A state must accord out-of-state citizens the same treatment as its own; but it is not required to give them special privileges. Thus it may not deny citizens of other states access to its courts, or deny them the equal protection of its laws, or tax them at discriminatory rates. On the other hand, political rights may be made to depend on residence, as also may the right to attend state-supported institutions. Formerly also, a state might exclude citizens of other states from fishing in its streams, and so on, but recent cases seem to call this doctrine into question.[3]

Section 2

2. A PERSON CHARGED IN ANY STATE WITH TREASON, FELONY, OR OTHER CRIME, WHO SHALL FLEE FROM JUSTICE, AND BE FOUND IN ANOTHER STATE, SHALL, ON DEMAND OF THE EXECUTIVE AUTHORITY OF THE STATE FROM WHICH HE FLED, BE DELIVERED UP, TO BE REMOVED TO THE STATE HAVING JURISDICTION OF THE CRIME.

This paragraph provides for what is known as "interstate rendition" or, more commonly, as "extradition." Despite its positive language, there is no judicial method of forcing a state to extradite fugitives from justice. In a celebrated case of this kind not many years ago the Governor of New Jersey refused to extradite a fugitive from a Georgia chain gang, and Georgia was helpless. In most cases, however, escaped prisoners are returned, under an old act of Congress, to the states *from* which they fled by the Governor of the state *to* which they fled.

Section 2

3. NO PERSON HELD TO SERVICE OR LABOUR IN ONE STATE, UNDER THE LAWS THEREOF, ESCAPING INTO ANOTHER, SHALL, IN CONSEQUENCE OF ANY LAW OR REGULATION THEREIN, BE DISCHARGED FROM SUCH SERVICE OR LABOUR, BUT SHALL BE DELIVERED UP ON CLAIM OF THE PARTY TO WHOM SUCH SERVICE OR LABOUR MAY BE DUE.

The Thirteenth Amendment, abolishing slavery, nullified this so-called "Fugitive Slave" clause.

Section 3

1. NEW STATES MAY BE ADMITTED BY THE CONGRESS INTO THIS UNION;

It is very probable that Hawaii, and possibly Alaska, will soon be admitted as states into this Union. The procedure normally used is as follows: (1) a petition by the inhabitants of a territory for admission to the Union; (2) a congressional resolution approved by the President authorizing the inhabitants of the territory to draw up a constitution; (3) approval of the proposed constitution by a majority of both houses of Congress and the President and admission of the territory into the Union.

While Congress and the President may withhold their approval of admission until the "state" complies with or agrees to certain conditions, yet once a state is admitted, it possesses the same political powers as the other states. For example, in 1910 President Taft vetoed legislation admitting Arizona to the Union because its proposed constitution permitted the voters to recall state judges. After deleting this clause Arizona was admitted, and promptly proceeded to restore the objectionable section. Since the right to determine the method of selection, tenure, and removal of its own judges is a political power enjoyed by all states, Arizona's power in this respect could not be less than that of other states; the condition was unenforceable.

On the other hand, conditions relating to the public lands in the state may be enforced as contracts which do not detract from a state's political power. Thus Minnesota agreed when admitted to the Union, in return for certain public lands which she received from the national government, not to tax land still owned in the state by the government. This agreement the Court enforced.[4]

The Civil War conclusively settled the question whether or not a state can constitutionally withdraw from the Union. In the words of the Supreme Court, ours is "an indestructible Union composed of indestructible States."[5]

Section 3

1. continued: BUT NO NEW STATE SHALL BE FORMED OR ERECTED WITHIN THE JURISDICTION OF ANY OTHER STATE; NOR ANY STATE BE FORMED BY THE JUNCTION OF TWO OR MORE STATES, OR PARTS OF STATES, WITHOUT THE CONSENT OF THE LEGISLATURES OF THE STATES CONCERNED AS WELL AS OF THE CONGRESS.

Five states have been formed or erected within the jurisdiction of some other state with the consent of the legislatures concerned and of Congress: Vermont from New York in 1791, Kentucky from Virginia in 1792, Tennessee from North Carolina in 1796, Maine from Massachusetts in 1820, and West Virginia from Virginia in 1863. At the time Texas was admitted to the Union, Congress consented to the division of the state into five states if the Texas legislature ever should so wish, but it seems never to have so wished, being indisposed to part with the distinction of being the largest state in the Union.

Section 3

2. THE CONGRESS SHALL HAVE POWER TO DISPOSE OF AND MAKE ALL NEEDFUL RULES AND REGULATIONS RE-

SPECTING THE TERRITORY OR OTHER PROPERTY BE-
LONGING TO THE UNITED STATES; AND NOTHING IN
THIS CONSTITUTION SHALL BE SO CONSTRUED AS TO
PREJUDICE ANY CLAIMS OF THE UNITED STATES,
OR OF ANY PARTICULAR STATE.

When Puerto Rico, the Philippines, and Hawaii were annexed, the question arose whether or not "the Constitution followed the flag." The chief difficulty sprang from the fact that the
new territories had not been molded in the political and legal
traditions back of the Constitution; and also that in certain areas
their inhabitants were only semicivilized. To apply all the
provisions of the Constitution in such conditions was out of the
question. For example, it would have necessitated the trial of
offenses by juries composed of illiterates, even of near savages.
Yet, if the Constitution did not apply, would not the inhabitants
be without any safeguards against arbitrary rule?

Although the Constitution itself did not offer a clear solution,
the Supreme Court met the problem by distinguishing between
fundamental and *formal* parts of the Constitution and by holding that in "*un*incorporated territories"* only the fundamental
provisions of the Constitution, those which guarantee fair trials,
freedom of speech, etc., applied, unless and until Congress provided otherwise.[6]

Section 4

1. THE UNITED STATES SHALL GUARANTEE TO EVERY
STATE IN THIS UNION A REPUBLICAN FORM OF
GOVERNMENT,

While the Constitution does not define "a republican form
of government," the framers undoubtedly meant a form which,
as distinguished from aristocracy, monarchy, or direct democracy, rested on the consent of the people and operated through

---

* Unincorporated territories are those which Congress has not explicitly or
impliedly made an integral part of the Union. At the present time, all territories except Hawaii and Alaska are unincorporated.

representative institutions. Interpretation of the clause belongs to Congress. If Congress permits the senators and representatives of a particular state to take their seats in Congress, that state must be deemed to have "a republican form of government" within the meaning of the Constitution. For example, in 1902 Oregon adopted the "initiative," whereby its citizens are enabled to legislate directly without the intervention of the legislature.* A company which had been taxed under a law passed by the initiative procedure argued that this transgressed the above provision; but the Court refused to intervene, holding that "violation of the . . . guaranty of a republican form of government . . . cannot be challenged in the courts."[7] Recently, however, opponents of the poll tax requirement for voting which exists in some of the Southern states have endeavored to get up a case in which the Court would be asked to say that the requirement was not in accord with "a republican form of government"; but so far all such endeavors have failed.

There are certain other questions arising under the Constitution that the Supreme Court will not answer, either because they are directed to the political branches of the government, the Congress and the President, or because they would involve the Court directly in political contests. Examples of such "political questions" can be found on pages 73, 75.

Section 4

1. continued: AND SHALL PROTECT EACH OF THEM AGAINST INVASION;

Invasion of a state by a foreign power would also be an invasion of the United States.

---

* Simply stated, the initiative procedure calls for two steps: (1) securing signatures of a required number of voters to a petition calling for submission of a proposed law to the electorate; (2) submission of the proposal to the voters in a general election. If approved by the voters, the proposal becomes law.

Section 4

1. continued: AND ON APPLICATION OF THE LEGISLA-
TURE, OR OF THE EXECUTIVE (WHEN THE LEGISLA-
TURE CANNOT BE CONVENED) AGAINST DOMESTIC
VIOLENCE.

Congress has delegated to the President the authority to send troops into a state to protect it from "domestic violence," on the request of the appropriate state authority. In 1842 there were two governments in Rhode Island, each of which claimed to be the legitimate one. When President Tyler indicated that he was prepared to send troops to defend one of these against the "domestic violence" of the other, he was at the same time determining which government was the legitimate one. The Supreme Court, in refusing to intervene, identified the question as "political" in nature.[8]

The President may also send troops into a state without the consent of state officials, even against their protests, if he finds it necessary to do so in order to enforce federal laws or to preserve the property or "the peace of the United States."[9]

Article V—The Amendatory Article

THE CONGRESS, WHENEVER TWO THIRDS OF BOTH HOUSES SHALL DEEM IT NECESSARY, SHALL PROPOSE AMENDMENTS TO THIS CONSTITUTION, OR, ON THE APPLICATION OF THE LEGISLATURES OF TWO THIRDS OF THE SEVERAL STATES, SHALL CALL A CONVENTION FOR PROPOSING AMENDMENTS, WHICH, IN EITHER CASE, SHALL BE VALID TO ALL INTENTS AND PURPOSES, AS PART OF THIS CONSTITUTION, WHEN RATIFIED BY THE LEGISLATURES OF THREE FOURTHS OF THE SEVERAL STATES, OR BY CONVENTIONS IN THREE FOURTHS THEREOF, AS THE ONE OR THE OTHER MODE OF RATIFICATION MAY BE PROPOSED BY THE CONGRESS;

An amendment must be both proposed and ratified before it becomes part of the Constitution. It may be proposed by a two-thirds vote of *both* houses of Congress (as all amendments have been proposed), or by a national convention called by Congress on the application of the legislatures of two thirds of the states. All twenty-one of the amendments so far added to the Constitution were proposed by Congress, as also were the two unratified ones still before the country (see pages 139–141). During the nullification crisis of 1832, however, and shortly prior to the Civil War several state legislatures petitioned for a national convention for a general revision of the Constitution, and from time to time scholars have suggested that a national constitutional convention be called to consider a complete overhauling of the Constitution from the point of view of modern needs, but so far without success. Although the word "shall" is used in connection with calling the convention, there would be no way to compel Congress to do so. In other words, the Constitution at this point, as at many others, relies for its observance on the good faith of Congress. The Constitution's silence as to the details of such a convention—the method of choosing delegates, the number of representatives from each state, and the power of the convention once assembled—apparently leaves it with Congress to determine these important matters.

Proposed amendments must be ratified by the legislatures of three fourths of the states (all amendments except the Twenty-first were ratified by this method) or by special state conventions of three fourths of the states. Congress decides which method of ratification shall be used. But if a constitutional convention should be called, there might be some question whether it or Congress should determine the method of ratification. The precedent of the Constitutional Convention of 1787 (see page 81) suggests that, when once assembled, a convention might establish an entirely new method of ratification and, indeed, propose an entirely new constitution. When Congress proposed the Twenty-first Amendment repealing Prohibition (see pages 137–138), it left it with each state to determine for itself the manner in which delegates to its ratifying convention should be chosen.

Although a state legislature, after voting against ratification, may change its mind and ratify, it may not withdraw a ratification once given. When three fourths of the states have ratified a proposed amendment, the Secretary of State, subject to the directions of Congress, promulgates the amendment and it thereupon becomes part of the Constitution. Amendments must be ratified within a "reasonable time" after they have been proposed. But in the absence of a congressionally established time limit, the courts will not determine what constitutes a "reasonable time." This is a political question which Congress decides when it instructs the Secretary of State whether or not to promulgate an amendment. When Congress proposed the Eighteenth, Twentieth, and Twenty-first Amendments, it stated that unless three fourths of the states ratified within seven years, the particular amendment would be inoperative. Many other questions, too, arising out of the amendatory article have been held by the Court to be political questions; indeed, it is probable that the present Court would, if occasion arose, accept Justice Black's statement a few years ago that "Congress, possessing exclusive power over the amending process, cannot be bound by and is under no duty to accept the pronouncements upon that exclusive power by this Court . . . "[1]

Between 1789 and 1949 approximately 4,500 amendments were introduced in Congress, but only twenty-eight amendments were actually proposed. Twenty-two of these have been ratified and two are still awaiting possible ratification (see pages 139–141). Two of the rejected amendments were proposed along with the ten that were finally ratified as the Bill of Rights (see page 86). Another proposal of amendment that was not ratified (1810) would have withdrawn citizenship from any person who accepted a title of nobility or who received without the consent of Congress an office or emolument from a foreign power. The latest proposal not to be ratified was one by Congress on the eve of the Civil War (1861) which would have prohibited any amendment to the Constitution interfering with slavery in any of the states. Four years later the Thirteenth Amendment forbade slavery throughout "the United States and all places subject to their jurisdiction" (see page 114).

Although the Constitution was written before the industrial and democratic revolutions had made their impress on the nation, it continues to serve as the fundamental law of a powerful industrial democracy. Obviously the Constitution has had to change as the nation changed. While the framework is the same, fundamental alterations have taken place in the actual operation of that framework, and the amending process has been relatively unimportant in this development; less formal and more subtle methods have been used. The Constitution was *democratized* by the extension of the suffrage within the states and the rise of national political parties. The national government has been rendered adequate to meet the exigencies of a national economy and of an interdependent world through wise *adaptation* and *interpretation* (legislative, executive, and judicial) of the Constitution. As the development of a national industrial economy has enlarged the scope, extent, and nature of interstate commerce, so have the powers of the national government been correspondingly increased. As the necessities of national defense have become more demanding, so have the powers and responsibilities of the national government grown.

The formal amendatory procedures have been criticized as "undemocratic." One fourth of the states (which could be less than one fourth of the people) can block amendments desired by an overwhelming majority of the country. On the other hand, it is possible for amendments to be adopted without a direct expression of popular opinion. The latter criticism would be largely met were Congress to require ratification by state conventions called for the purpose rather than by state legislatures chosen on other issues.*

PROVIDED THAT NO AMENDMENT WHICH MAY BE MADE PRIOR TO THE YEAR ONE THOUSAND EIGHT HUNDRED AND EIGHT SHALL IN ANY MANNER AFFECT THE FIRST AND FOURTH CLAUSES IN THE NINTH SECTION OF THE FIRST ARTICLE;

* The Constitution can be constitutionally changed only through the amendatory procedures and the less formal methods described above, but the people always retain the right of revolution. This is not a constitutional or legal right, and it is one that every citizen exercises at his own peril since the government has the duty to protect and preserve itself. The right of revolution is set forth in its most classic form by the Declaration of Independence in the following words: "That to secure these rights [life, liberty, and the pursuit of happiness] governments are instituted among men, deriving their just powers from the consent of the governed, that whenever any form of government becomes destructive of these ends, it is the right of the people to alter or to abolish it, and institute new government, laying its foundations on such principles, and organizing its powers in such form as to them shall seem most likely to effect their safety and happiness." The Declaration does not uphold the right of a minority to revolt in order to oppress the majority; it is the right of the majority to alter or abolish its own government when necessary, and only when necessary, to protect their "unalienable rights."

This provision referred to the importation of slaves and has only historical interest today.

> AND [provided] THAT NO STATE, WITHOUT ITS CONSENT, SHALL BE DEPRIVED OF ITS EQUAL SUFFRAGE IN THE SENATE.

This is the only provision of the entire Constitution which some consider unamendable. But others contend that there are ways in which even this can be changed. It could be repealed by amendment and then another amendment could be adopted by the regular procedure which would permit unequal representation in the Senate.

Article VI—The Supremacy Article

Section 1

1. ALL DEBTS CONTRACTED AND ENGAGEMENTS ENTERED
INTO, BEFORE THE ADOPTION OF THIS CONSTITUTION,
SHALL BE AS VALID AGAINST THE UNITED STATES UNDER
THIS CONSTITUTION, AS UNDER THE CONFEDERATION.

At the time of the Constitutional Convention the securities
and currency issued by the Confederation and the several states
had depreciated in value. Later Alexander Hamilton, Washington's brilliant Secretary of the Treasury, proposed that the
national government assume the debts of the several states and
pay in full the debts of the Confederation. Adoption of this
proposal did much to strengthen the new Union—at a handsome
profit to speculators in Confederation securities.

Section 2

1. THIS CONSTITUTION, AND THE LAWS OF THE UNITED
STATES WHICH SHALL BE MADE IN PURSUANCE
THEREOF; AND ALL TREATIES MADE, OR WHICH SHALL
BE MADE, UNDER THE AUTHORITY OF THE UNITED
STATES, SHALL BE THE SUPREME LAW OF THE LAND;
AND THE JUDGES IN EVERY STATE SHALL BE BOUND
THEREBY, ANY THING IN THE CONSTITUTION OR LAWS
OF ANY STATE TO THE CONTRARY NOTWITHSTANDING.

This clause lays down one of the key principles of the Constitution. It makes federalism work. *The powers of the national
government are limited, but within the field of its powers it is*

supreme, and this supremacy the state courts are bound to uphold. Any provision of a state constitution or any state law is null and void when it conflicts with the Constitution, a federal law passed in pursuance of the Constitution, or a treaty made under the authority of the United States. For a single example out of scores and dozens, in 1941 the Supreme Court held that a Pennsylvania law to regulate the activities of enemy aliens was unconstitutional on the ground that it conflicted with the federal Alien Registration Law.[1]

The treaty-making power of the national government is broader than its legislative power. Laws must be made *in pursuance of the Constitution* in order to be the supreme law of the land, but treaties have only to be made *under the authority of the United States*. When in 1913 Congress regulated by law the hunting of migratory birds, the law was held to be unconstitutional on the ground that it went beyond the scope of the national government's legislative powers. Three years later the United States became party to a treaty with Great Britain in which the national government agreed to protect birds which migrated between Canada and this country. In order to fulfill the obligations of the United States under this treaty, Congress passed a law much more stringent than the 1913 regulation, and this law the Court upheld.[2]

The treaty-making power is not unlimited, however. It has to be exercised in a particular way, and it cannot be used to deprive citizens of the United States of their constitutional rights.

Section 3

1. THE SENATORS AND REPRESENTATIVES BEFORE MENTIONED, AND THE MEMBERS OF THE SEVERAL STATE LEGISLATURES, AND ALL EXECUTIVE AND JUDICIAL OFFICERS, BOTH OF THE UNITED STATES AND OF THE SEVERAL STATES, SHALL BE BOUND BY OATH OR AFFIRMATION, TO SUPPORT THIS CONSTITUTION; BUT NO RELIGIOUS TEST SHALL EVER BE REQUIRED AS A QUALIFICATION TO ANY OFFICE OR PUBLIC TRUST UNDER THE UNITED STATES.

Article VII—Ratification of the Constitution

Section 1

1. THE RATIFICATION OF THE CONVENTIONS OF NINE STATES, SHALL BE SUFFICIENT FOR THE ESTABLISHMENT OF THIS CONSTITUTION BETWEEN THE STATES SO RATIFYING THE SAME.

The Constitutional Convention was a revolutionary body. The delegates were representatives of the states acting in response to a call by the Congress of the Confederation. Since the Articles of Confederation could be amended only with the consent of all thirteen state legislatures, and since they created a "perpetual Union," Congress, when it called the Convention, had explicitly stated that no recommendations should be effective until approved by Congress and ratified in accordance with the terms of the Articles—that is, by all *thirteen state legislatures*. Nevertheless the delegates to the Convention boldly assumed power to exceed their mandate and to propose an entirely new government which was to go into effect upon the ratification by specially chosen *conventions of only nine of the thirteen states.*

DONE IN CONVENTION BY THE UNANIMOUS CONSENT OF THE STATES PRESENT THE SEVENTEENTH DAY OF SEPTEMBER IN THE YEAR OF OUR LORD ONE THOUSAND SEVEN HUNDRED AND EIGHTY SEVEN AND OF THE INDEPENDENCE OF THE UNITED STATES OF AMERICA THE TWELFTH IN WITNESS WHEREOF WE HAVE HEREUNTO SUBSCRIBED OUR NAMES,

This ambiguous form was accepted on the advice of Gouverneur Morris and Benjamin Franklin. It permitted delegates to attest that the Constitution was the unanimous act of "the States present" without pledging themselves to support it in the ensuing ratification struggle. Despite this form three members present refused to sign, Elbridge Gerry of Massachusetts, Edmund Randolph and George Mason of Virginia. Others who opposed the Constitution had already left the Convention, and Rhode Island had refused to send delegates in the first place.*

Go. Washington—
Presidt and deputy from Virginia

NEW HAMPSHIRE

John Langdon	Nicholas Gilman

MASSACHUSETTS

Nathaniel Gorham	Rufus King

CONNECTICUT

Wm. Saml. Johnson	Roger Sherman

NEW YORK

Alexander Hamilton	

NEW JERSEY

Wil: Livingston	David Brearley
Wm. Paterson	Jona. Dayton

PENNSYLVANIA

B Franklin	Thomas Mifflin
Robt. Morris	Geo. Clymer
Thos FitzSimons	Jared Ingersoll
James Wilson	Gouv Morris

DELAWARE

Geo: Read	Gunning Bedford jun
John Dickinson	Richard Bassett
Jaco: Broom	

MARYLAND

James McHenry	Dan of St. Thos. Jenifer
Danl. Carroll	

VIRGINIA

John Blair	James Madison Jr.

* Much of the time New York was unrepresented.

Wm. Blount   Richd. Dobbs Spaight
Hu Williamson

SOUTH CAROLINA

J. Rutledge   Charles Cotesworth Pinckney
Charles Pinckney   Pierce Butler

GEORGIA

William Few   Abr Baldwin
            Attest: WILLIAM JACKSON, Secretary

Seventy-four persons had been appointed delegates, but only fifty-five attended, of whom only thirty-nine took a serious part in the deliberations. This distinguished gathering of statesmen was not interested in mere political speculation but, above everything else, in establishing a government that would work. They were well equipped for the task; seven of them had served as Governor of their respective states, thirty-nine had served in Congress, eight had had previous experience in constitution-making within their own states. Despite this wealth of experience, it is interesting to note that the Convention was composed mainly of comparatively young men. The youngest was only twenty-six, six were under thirty-one, and only twelve were over fifty-four. They were all men of consequence—merchants, manufacturers, planters, bankers, lawyers. The small farmers and city mechanics were not represented and the back-country rural areas were greatly underrepresented, although this was not the case in several of the state ratifying conventions.

Conspicuous by reason of their absence from the Convention were Patrick Henry, Samuel Adams, John Adams, John Hancock, Tom Paine, and Thomas Jefferson—the fiery democratic leaders of the Revolution. Henry had been appointed but refused to attend; he was not in favor of revising the Articles of Confederation. "I smelt a rat," he is reported to have remarked. Jefferson and John Adams were abroad, representing the United States in a diplomatic capacity, Paine had returned to England, and Hancock and Samuel Adams had not been chosen delegates.

Six men stand out as leaders of the Convention: General Washington, James Madison, Edmund Randolph, Benjamin Franklin,

James Wilson, and Gouveneur Morris—three from Virginia, three from Pennsylvania.

Washington, first citizen of Virginia and of the United States, was unanimously selected to preside over the Convention. He had been extremely reluctant to attend, and accepted only when persuaded that his prestige was needed to assure the success of the Convention. Although he seldom spoke, his influence was vitally felt both in informal gatherings and in the Convention sessions. The universal assumption that he would become the first President under the new government inspired confidence in it.

Madison, only thirty-six at the time of the Convention, was one of the most learned and informed of the delegates. He had been a member both of the Congress and the Virginia Assembly. Foreseeing the probable future significance of the Convention, Madison always sat in the front of the room where he could hear all that was said and kept a detailed record of the proceedings. Even today *Madison's Notes* remains our major source of information concerning the Convention.

Edmund Randolph, although only thirty-four, was Governor of Virginia at the time of the Convention, and a member of one of Virginia's first families. Although he declined to sign the Constitution, he later advocated its ratification.

Benjamin Franklin, at eighty-one, was the Convention's oldest member. Second only to Washington in the esteem of his countrymen, Franklin had a firm faith in the people. Despite his great age Franklin played an active role in the Convention. At critical moments his sagacious and humorous remarks broke the tension and prevented bitterness.

Most of Franklin's speeches were read by his fellow delegate, James Wilson. This Scottish-born and Scottish-trained lawyer had signed the Declaration of Independence and represented his state in Congress. He was a strong supporter of Madison, and his work on the Convention's Committee on Detail, although inconspicuous, was very important.

In sharp contrast to Franklin, the third Pennsylvania delegate, Gouverneur Morris, was strongly aristocratic in his sympathies. He was an eloquent and interesting speaker, and addressed the

Convention more often than any other member; and his facility with the pen is shown by the fact that he was chosen to write the final draft of the Constitution. Years later he began a letter, "The hand that writes this letter wrote the Constitution."

Besides these six there were several others of outstanding prominence in the Convention: George Mason, Charles Pinckney, Roger Sherman, Alexander Hamilton, Luther Martin, to mention a few. Hamilton, representing New York, did not, however, play as important a role as one might expect, his influence being nullified to a great extent by associates who opposed the Constitution. Hamilton lost influence, also, through his advocacy of an extremely strong and centralized national government. At the opposite extreme was Luther Martin from Maryland who was an ardent and fearfully boring champion of the small states. As soon as it was apparent that his views were in the minority, Luther went back to Maryland.

The Constitution was ratified by the conventions in the several states as follows: Delaware, December 7, 1787; Pennsylvania, December 12, 1787; New Jersey, December 18, 1787; Georgia, January 2, 1788; Connecticut, January 9, 1788; Massachusetts, February 6, 1788; Maryland, April 28, 1788; South Carolina, May 23, 1788; New Hampshire, June 21, 1788; Virginia, June 26, 1788; New York, July 26, 1788; North Carolina, November 21, 1789; Rhode Island, May 29, 1790.

Amendments

The Bill of Rights

Although the first eight amendments differ in character from Amendments IX and X, all are commonly grouped together as the Bill of Rights. Much of the opposition to the ratification of the Constitution stemmed from its lack of specific guarantees of certain fundamental rights. The Constitutional Convention failed to adopt such guarantees because it was thought to be both unnecessary and dangerous—unnecessary because the Constitution itself prohibited bills of attainder, ex post facto laws, suspension of the writ of habeas corpus except in times of public danger, and required trial by jury in federal criminal cases; dangerous because prohibitions might furnish an argument for claiming powers not granted the new government. Thus to forbid the national government to *abridge* freedom of the press might be thought to imply that it had the power to *regulate* the press if it could do so without abridging it. It was also urged that the protection of fundamental rights ultimately rested not on paper guarantees, but in the hearts and minds of the nation's citizens.[1]

Despite these arguments there was a general demand for a Bill of Rights, and the Constitution was adopted with the understanding that the first business of the First Congress would be the consideration of suitable amendments. Congress proposed twelve such amendments on September 25, 1789; ten were ratified and became part of the Constitution on December 15, 1791. The two failing of ratification prescribed the ratio of representation to population in the House of Representatives and prohibited any increase in congressmen's compensation until an election for representatives had intervened.

Amendment I—Religion, Speech, Assembly, Petition

Proposed September 25, 1789—Ratified December 15, 1791

CONGRESS SHALL MAKE NO LAW RESPECTING AN ESTAB-
LISHMENT OF RELIGION,

Although the First Amendment is directed specifically to Congress, interpretation of the Fourteenth Amendment has now
made it, for the most part, applicable to the states (see pages
118–120).

God is not mentioned in the Constitution, and the word "religion" occurs in only one other place—in the prohibition of any
religious test as a qualification for office. The framers were not
irreligious; several of them came from states with *established
religions*, but all were probably in agreement that such matters
ought not to fall to the jurisdiction of the national government.
What things does the ban on "an establishment of religion" rule
out today? Certainly, governmental favoritism for any particular
religion; perhaps any considerable amount of *direct* governmental aid for religion in general. But neither tax exemption for
property owned by churches or used for religious purposes nor
expenditure of public moneys for chaplains for legislatures and
the armed services has ever been construed to violate the ban.
Moreover, the Supreme Court has in recent years upheld state
and local governments in furnishing free textbooks, free lunches,
and free transportation to pupils of Catholic parochial schools,
along with similar benefactions to pupils of the public schools.[2]

But these holdings were based on the interest of the state in promoting the education, health, and safety of its children, *not* in promoting their instruction in religion. The parochial school, in short, was regarded as a distributing agent for welfare services.

On the other hand, public schools are clearly prohibited from teaching any particular religion, and unless the Court qualifies a recent decision (1948), they may not permit privately selected teachers to use public schoolrooms for religious instruction.[3] Remembering that in 1789 an "establishment of religion" meant a state church, like the Church of England, this decision seems to be rather farfetched.

OR PROHIBITING THE FREE EXERCISE THEREOF;

Since there can be no compulsion by law of any form of worship, and since the government recognizes neither orthodoxy nor heresy, everyone has an absolute right to believe whatever he wishes. Although carefully protected, the right to act in accordance with one's belief is not, and cannot be, absolute. Religion may not sanction action or a refusal to act if either is harmful to the safety, morals, health, or general welfare of the community. No one has a right to refuse "to bear arms,"* to refuse to pay taxes, to practice polygamy, or to invade the rights of others even in the name of religion.

The importance of religious freedom has been re-emphasized by the Supreme Court within the last several years in a series of decisions arising out of the activities of the Jehovah's Witnesses. The Witnesses assert that organized religion is "a racket" and that it is their duty to expose it by distributing literature, ringing doorbells, playing records, setting up public address systems in the public parks, and so on. The Supreme Court has held that the right to proselytize in these ways is part of religious freedom and cannot be curtailed or limited by the requirement of licenses or prior approval of public officials.[4] In two important Witnesses

* During World Wars I and II Congress exempted from military duty persons who by reason of religious training and belief were conscientiously opposed to participation in war. This privilege was one granted by Congress but not required by the Constitution.

cases, the Court first held that public school pupils may be forced to salute the flag (which is to the Witnesses a symbol of the Evil One); and then held the opposite.[5]

OR ABRIDGING THE FREEDOM OF SPEECH, OR OF THE PRESS;

The right of freedom of speech and press is essential to the preservation and operation of democracy, but even this right is not absolute. Anyone who slanders or libels another may be penalized, slander being an oral statement which maliciously or falsely defames or injures another, while a libel is a written statement of like nature.

Also, freedom of speech and press is subject to restraint and punishment whenever there is a "clear and present danger" that exercise of the right would lead to an evil which a government has the right to prevent. For example, if someone should advise persons to refuse to register for the draft under circumstances that made it highly likely that draft evasions would actually result (a substantive evil which the government has the right to prevent), he could be enjoined from speaking or writing in such a fashion, and punished if he did so.[6]

But how about the advocacy of sedition, sedition itself being punishable? The answer appears to be that if the advocacy occurs under such circumstances that there is, in the judgment of five justices of the Supreme Court, "a clear and present danger" that it will lead to seditious acts, it can be prevented and punished.

In other words, as this doctrine is presently applied, it is the Supreme Court of the United States rather than legislative bodies which determines whether a danger is sufficiently clear and present to justify a curtailment of speech or press.[7]

The right to speak through *peaceful* picketing is guaranteed by this Amendment and cannot be prohibited except as the clear-and-present-danger test applies. But picketing which is accompanied by threats and violence is not free speech and cannot claim constitutional protection as such.

OR THE RIGHT OF THE PEOPLE PEACEABLY TO ASSEMBLE, AND TO PETITION THE GOVERNMENT FOR A REDRESS OF GRIEVANCES.

Public meetings may be regulated in the general interest. A public assembly in a crowded business district at the busy noon hour, for example, could be prohibited without violating the First Amendment (or Fourteenth). But protection of the public may not be used as an excuse to prevent peaceable assembly, and the courts will scrutinize such regulations when a case is brought before them.

Amendment II—Militia and the Right to Bear Arms

Proposed September 25, 1789—Ratified December 15, 1791

A WELL REGULATED MILITIA, BEING NECESSARY TO THE SECURITY OF A FREE STATE,* THE RIGHT OF THE PEOPLE TO KEEP AND BEAR ARMS, SHALL NOT BE INFRINGED.

The fear that Congress might disarm the state militias prompted this Amendment. The right to bear arms is for the sole purpose of maintaining a militia and does not prohibit Congress from taxing heavily the sale and use by private individuals of certain types of weapons, like sawed-off shotguns.

* This refers to state in the generic sense rather than to states of this Union.

Amendment III—Quartering of Soldiers

Proposed September 25, 1789—Ratified December 15, 1791

NO SOLDIER SHALL, IN TIME OF PEACE BE QUARTERED IN
ANY HOUSE, WITHOUT THE CONSENT OF THE OWNER, NOR
IN TIME OF WAR, BUT IN A MANNER TO BE PRESCRIBED BY
LAW.

Certain remarks of Justice Miller are here appropriate: "This
amendment seems to have been thought necessary. It does not
appear to have been the subject of judicial exposition; and it is so
thoroughly in accord with all our ideas, that further comment is
unnecessary."[8]

Amendment IV—Searches and Seizures

Proposed September 25, 1789—Ratified December 15, 1791

THE RIGHT OF THE PEOPLE TO BE SECURE IN THEIR PER-
SONS, HOUSES, PAPERS, AND EFFECTS, AGAINST UNREASON-
ABLE SEARCHES AND SEIZURES, SHALL NOT BE VIOLATED,
AND NO WARRANTS SHALL ISSUE, BUT UPON PROBABLE
CAUSE, SUPPORTED BY OATH OR AFFIRMATION, AND PAR-
TICULARLY DESCRIBING THE PLACE TO BE SEARCHED, AND
THE PERSONS OR THINGS TO BE SEIZED. [See page 96.]

It is *unreasonable* searches and seizures which are prohibited. In general, a search and seizure is unreasonable when it takes place without a warrant. But a search may be conducted without a warrant if it is contemporary with and incidental to a lawful arrest, and also in the case of vehicles suspected of carrying stolen or illegal goods. How strictly the Court has sometimes construed this Amendment may be illustrated by the fact that a search without our warrant and subsequent arrest was held unconstitutional even though the odor of opium emanated from the room involved and a single occupant was found in it.[9]

Corporations, like individuals, are protected, but law enforcement officers are permitted greater leeway in searching corporate papers than in searching the effects of individuals. Also, a person's house and private papers are entitled to greater protection than his place of business and his business papers.

This Amendment is interpreted in conjunction with that clause of Amendment V which protects anyone from testifying against himself in federal criminal cases. When personal effects of an accused person are unconstitutionally seized they may not be used as evidence against him, otherwise he would be forced to testify against himself. But while this is the doctrine of the United States Supreme Court, the majority of state courts hold that such evidence is valid.

Amendment V—Grand Juries, Double Jeopardy, Self-Incrimination, Due Process, Eminent Domain

Proposed September 25, 1789—Ratified December 15, 1791

NO PERSON SHALL BE HELD TO ANSWER FOR A CAPITAL, OR OTHERWISE INFAMOUS CRIME, UNLESS ON A PRESENT-MENT OR INDICTMENT OF A GRAND JURY, EXCEPT IN CASES ARISING IN THE LAND OR NAVAL FORCES, OR IN THE MILITIA, WHEN IN ACTUAL SERVICE IN TIME OF WAR OR PUBLIC DANGER;

Amendment V introduces us to the most ancient institution known to the Constitution, the *Grand Jury*. It hails from the days of William the Conqueror, and the trial, or petty (also spelled petit) jury is an offshoot from it. (See Amendment VI.) Like its English forerunner, the grand jury is composed of not more than twenty-three members of whom twelve are sufficient to make a "presentment" or return an "indictment," that is, to accuse some person or persons of an offense against the laws of the United States, either on the basis of evidence gathered by itself or of evidence laid before it by a prosecuting officer. Since the "accused" is not being tried, the grand jury's proceedings are secret and one-sided (*ex parte*), only the government being represented.*

NOR SHALL ANY PERSON BE SUBJECT FOR THE SAME OF-
FENSE TO BE TWICE PUT IN JEOPARDY OF LIFE OR LIMB;

A person has been put in jeopardy as soon as a properly con-
stituted jury has been sworn and some evidence submitted against
him. If, however, a jury is dismissed because it is composed of
persons not competent to serve, the accused was never in
jeopardy and may be tried before another jury. Several "offenses" may arise from the same act and a person may be placed
in jeopardy for each of the offenses. The test of whether or not
an offense is "the same offense" is whether the same evidence is
required to sustain conviction.

Also, the same act, e.g., selling narcotics, may be an offense
against both the national and the state governments, but a trial
by the state does not prevent a subsequent trial by the national
government, and vice versa. Neither does the restriction on
double jeopardy prevent civil in addition to criminal proceedings, nor a retrial on motion of the accused himself.

NOR SHALL BE COMPELLED IN ANY CRIMINAL CASE TO BE
A WITNESS AGAINST HIMSELF,

This provision has been greatly broadened by judicial interpretation. Originally it meant only that *a person under trial* might
not be forced to testify against himself. Today it means that no
person may be compelled by *any governmental agency*—the
House Committee on Un-American Activities, for instance, or
the Federal Trade Commission—to answer *under oath* any ques-

---

* During a recent trial in Georgia, (January, 1949) of two white men who
were accused of having murdered a Negro, two members of the trial jury
stepped down from the jury box and testified under oath to their belief in the
good character of the accused persons. This occurrence seems shocking today,
when "impartiality" is supposed to be the chief requirement of a juror. The
Georgia practice harks back to the time, four or five hundred years ago, when
the trial (petit) jury was not yet distinct from the grand jury and when the
latter often based its accusations on the personal knowledge of its members.

tion if, *according to his own claim,* his answer would "tend to incriminate him."[10]

NOR BE DEPRIVED OF LIFE, LIBERTY, OR PROPERTY, WITH-
OUT DUE PROCESS OF LAW;

A parallel clause is found in the Fourteenth Amendment (see pages 118–119) as a limitation on the states. The "due process" clauses of the Fifth and Fourteenth Amendments have resulted in more cases and controversies than any other in the Constitution except possibly the "commerce" clause and, earlier, the "obligation of contracts" clause (see page 37). Even so, it is impossible to give these clauses any exact, final, and completely satisfactory explanation. Indeed, the Supreme Court itself has refused to give them precise definition, stating that it preferred to rely upon "the gradual process of judicial inclusion and exclusion."[11] The fact is, however, that the longer this process has been continued, the vaguer the subject has become. Certain things, nevertheless, may be said concerning it with some assurance.

There are two kinds of due process—*procedural and substantive*. Procedural due process refers to the methods by which the law is enforced. It requires, to paraphrase Daniel Webster's famous definition, a procedure which "hears before it condemns, proceeds upon inquiry, and renders judgment only after [a] trial" in which the essentials of justice have been preserved.

A law itself may violate procedural due process if it fails to establish a definite standard of guilt or provide for fair procedures. For example, a New York statute which made it a crime to publish or distribute stories of crime, bloodshed, and lust so massed as to render them vehicles for inciting violence was held to be repugnant to the "due process" clause of the Fourteenth Amendment because it did not establish "an ascertainable standard of guilt"—in other words, did not make clear what was forbidden.[12] In the words of the Supreme Court: "A statute which either forbids or requires the doing of an act in terms so vague that men of common intelligence must necessarily guess at its meaning and differ as to its application, violates the first essential of due process of law."[13]

But for the most part procedural due process has its application in the courtroom. For the federal courts procedural due process requires at a minimum the careful observance of the Bill of Rights, especially Amendments IV through VIII. The national government must indict by grand jury, provide counsel for defendants in capital cases, not place any person in double jeopardy, etc. States, on the other hand, are restrained only by the more general "due process" clause of Amendment XIV (see pages 118–119).

Whereas *procedural* due process places limits on the *manner* in which governmental power may be exercised, *substantive* due process withdraws certain *subjects* from the full reach of governmental power regardless of the procedures used. Substantive due process, which began to be important in the United States Supreme Court about 1890, requires that the Court be convinced that the law—not merely the procedures by which the law would be enforced, but its very purpose—is *fair, reasonable,* and *just.*

Along with substantive due process the Supreme Court has also expanded the meaning of "property" and of "liberty," but especially of the latter. Originally "liberty" had meant "freedom from physical restraint," but now it has been expanded to denote "not merely freedom from bodily restraint, but also the right of the individual to contract, to engage in any of the common occupations of life, to acquire useful knowledge, to marry, establish a home and bring up children, to worship God according to the dictates of his own conscience, and generally to enjoy those privileges long recognized at common law as essential to the orderly pursuit of happiness by free men."[14]

Prior to 1937 the most important phase of this "new liberty" protected by the Supreme Court was "liberty of contract," that is, business liberty. Indeed, the adoption of the doctrine of substantive due process and the simultaneous expansion of the meaning of liberty rendered the Supreme Court for a time the final arbiter of our economic and industrial life. During this period the Court struck down many laws, laws regulating hours of labor, establishing minimum wages, regulating prices, outlawing unfair labor practices, and so on, on the ground that they were unreasonable interferences with the liberty of employers and employees to contract with one another.

Since 1937, however, the Supreme Court has largely abandoned the doctrine of "liberty of contract" and in general has refused to apply the doctrine of substantive due process to laws regulating the American economy. But this action did not presage a return to the old narrow conception of liberty or the abandonment of substantive due process. Quite to the contrary; since 1937 the word "liberty" of the Fifth and Fourteenth Amendments has been expanded to include the basic "civil liberties," and substantive due process has been given new life as a limitation of governmental power in the field of those liberties (see pages 118–119).[15]

NOR SHALL PRIVATE PROPERTY BE TAKEN FOR PUBLIC USE, WITHOUT JUST COMPENSATION.

This clause places a restriction on the national government's power of eminent domain, i.e., the power to take private property for public use, a power existing in all governments; for even in those which are organized on the principle of private ownership, the rights of society are paramount to those of any one owner. But private property may be taken under the eminent-domain power only for *public* use, and the owner must be fairly compensated. In cases of disagreement between the government and the individual as to what price is just, decision is referred to a disinterested body.

The "taking" mentioned in the clause must be "direct." The clause does not require that property losses incidental to the exercise of governmental powers be compensated for. Thus, the passage of a rent control measure would deprive persons of the right to charge what the traffic will bear and so decrease, presumably, the value of their property, but the government is not required to award compensation. Nor is it required to reimburse people for the losses which they may suffer because Congress lowers the tariff or declares war.

Amendment VI—Federal Criminal Court Procedures

Proposed September 25, 1789—Ratified December 15, 1791

IN ALL CRIMINAL PROSECUTIONS, THE ACCUSED SHALL ENJOY THE RIGHT TO A SPEEDY AND PUBLIC TRIAL, BY AN IMPARTIAL JURY OF THE STATE AND DISTRICT WHEREIN THE CRIME SHALL HAVE BEEN COMMITTED, WHICH DISTRICT SHALL HAVE BEEN PREVIOUSLY ASCERTAINED BY LAW, AND TO BE INFORMED OF THE NATURE AND CAUSE OF THE ACCUSATION; TO BE CONFRONTED WITH THE WITNESSES AGAINST HIM; TO HAVE COMPULSORY PROCESS FOR OBTAINING WITNESSES IN HIS FAVOR, AND TO HAVE THE ASSISTANCE OF COUNSEL FOR HIS DEFENSE.

The early English juries were always from the neighborhood, which was sometimes an advantage to an accused person, sometimes the contrary. The above provisions reflect this early requirement. A trial is "speedy" in a legal sense, which admits of considerable delays, especially those which are cooked up by counsel of the accused. An "impartial" jury used to be one from which the relatives and enemies of the accused were excluded; also those who admitted holding strong views about the pending case. Nowadays, however, questions of racial, religious, economic, and political connections are apt to be raised as bearing on the question of impartiality. The idea is sound enough if not pressed too far. Hardly anyone would contend that a jury trying a person accused of murder ought to have at least one murderer on it.

A defendant in a federal criminal case must be furnished a copy of the indictment and along with it a bill of the particular charges against him in order to enable him to prepare his defense. All testimony against him must be presented orally in court since he has the right to be confronted with the witnesses against him and to cross-examine them.* Also, the court must issue subpoenas requiring the presence of anyone whom the defendant wishes to testify. The court must also see that the defendant has the assistance of counsel, inform him of his right to the same, and secure counsel for him if he is unable to obtain it himself; but this right may be waived by a defendant in certain instances.

* Certain death-bed statements are an exception to this rule.

Amendment VII—Trial by Jury in Common Law Cases

Proposed September 25, 1789—Ratified December 15, 1791

IN SUITS AT COMMON LAW, WHERE THE VALUE IN CONTROVERSY SHALL EXCEED TWENTY DOLLARS, THE RIGHT OF TRIAL BY JURY SHALL BE PRESERVED, AND NO FACT TRIED BY A JURY, SHALL BE OTHERWISE RE-EXAMINED IN ANY COURT OF THE UNITED STATES, THAN ACCORDING TO THE RULES OF THE COMMON LAW.

This provision refers, of course, to litigation in the federal courts. It concerns suits at common law and does not prevent the two parties from dispensing with a jury with the consent of the court. Nor does it apply to equity proceedings, which are seldom before a jury, or to suits arising out of *statutory* law.

Amendment VIII—Bail, Cruel and Unusual Punishments

Proposed September 25, 1789—Ratified December 15, 1791

EXCESSIVE BAIL SHALL NOT BE REQUIRED, NOR EXCESSIVE FINES IMPOSED, NOR CRUEL AND UNUSUAL PUNISHMENTS INFLICTED.

Whether or not bail is "excessive" depends upon the nature of the offense, the reputation of the offender, and his ability to pay. A punishment is "cruel and unusual" if it is shocking to the sense of justice of the civilized world, a question also left with the Court. Death is not a cruel and unusual punishment when inflicted by hanging, electrocution, lethal gas, or a firing squad.

Amendment IX—Rights Retained by the People

Proposed September 25, 1789—Ratified December 15, 1791

THE ENUMERATION IN THE CONSTITUTION, OF CERTAIN RIGHTS, SHALL NOT BE CONSTRUED TO DENY OR DISPARAGE OTHERS RETAINED BY THE PEOPLE.

This Amendment embodies the dominant political thought of eighteenth-century America, which taught that before the establishment of government men existed in a state of nature and lived under the natural law which endowed them with certain natural rights. When, by mutual consent, men created government, they granted to it their natural right of judging and executing the natural law, but retained the rest of their natural rights. In accordance with this theory, the Bill of Rights did not *confer* rights, but merely *protected* those already granted by the natural law. This Amendment made it clear that the enumeration of rights to be protected against federal power did not imply that the other natural rights not mentioned were abandoned.

These supposed unenumerated rights have never been specified, and no law has ever been declared unconstitutional because of denial or disparagement of them.

Amendment X—Reserved Powers of the States

Proposed September 25, 1789—Ratified December 15, 1791

THE POWERS NOT DELEGATED TO THE UNITED STATES BY THE CONSTITUTION, NOR PROHIBITED BY IT TO THE STATES, ARE RESERVED TO THE STATES RESPECTIVELY, OR TO THE PEOPLE.

The term "reserved powers" in this Amendment makes it clear that the states, unlike the national government, do not owe their powers to the Constitution of the United States, but to their own constitutions. But, because of the "supremacy" clause (see page 79), such powers do not limit those of the national government or hamper their exercise—a point much insisted upon by Chief Justice Marshall. For one hundred years after Marshall's death, nevertheless, the Supreme Court from time to time held that *some* of the "reserved" powers of the states were "sovereign" powers, and hence set a limit to the delegated powers of the national government. Thus, when the latter used its clearly granted taxing and spending powers in such a way that agricultural production was regulated, its action was held by the Court, in 1937, to be repugnant to this Amendment, regulation of agriculture having been previously a concern of the states.[16]

Subsequently, however, the Court has returned to Marshall's point of view. Today it makes no difference constitutionally whether or not an act of Congress governs matters which were previously governed exclusively by the states.[17]

Amendment XI—Suits against States

Proposed March 4, 1794—Proclaimed January 8, 1798

THE JUDICIAL POWER OF THE UNITED STATES SHALL NOT BE CONSTRUED TO EXTEND TO ANY SUIT IN LAW OR EQUITY, COMMENCED OR PROSECUTED AGAINST ONE OF THE UNITED STATES BY CITIZENS OF ANOTHER STATE, OR BY CITIZENS OR SUBJECTS OF ANY FOREIGN STATES.

Article III, Section 2, paragraph 1 (see page 59), among other things extends the judicial power of the United States to "cases and controversies between a state and citizens of another state." During the struggle over ratification of the Constitution, many persons objected to this clause on the ground that it would permit a private individual to hale a state before a federal court, but were assured by Hamilton and others that because of the doctrine of "sovereign immunity," no state could ever be sued without its own consent. However, in 1792 the Supreme Court applied the literal terms of the Constitution and upheld the right of the federal courts to take jurisdiction in a case commenced by a citizen of South Carolina against Georgia.[18] Since many states were in default on their debts, there was great alarm lest a series of similar suits would result. Immediately after the Supreme Court's decision, the Eleventh Amendment was proposed, and its ratification in effect "recalled" the decision.

However, Amendment XI does not prevent an appeal from

the highest court of a state to the Supreme Court. Nor does it prevent federal courts, on the application of private individuals in appropriate proceedings, from restraining state officers who are acting unconstitutionally; by the principle of "the rule of law" an officer who acts beyond the law ceases to be an officer and thus ceases to be a representative of his state.

Amendment XII—Election of the President

Proposed December 8, 1803—Declared in force by the Secretary of State September 25, 1804

THE ELECTORS SHALL MEET IN THEIR RESPECTIVE STATES, AND VOTE BY BALLOT FOR PRESIDENT AND VICE-PRESIDENT, ONE OF WHOM, AT LEAST, SHALL NOT BE AN INHABITANT OF THE SAME STATE WITH THEMSELVES; THEY SHALL NAME IN THEIR BALLOTS THE PERSON VOTED FOR AS PRESIDENT, AND IN DISTINCT BALLOTS THE PERSON VOTED FOR AS VICE-PRESIDENT, AND THEY SHALL MAKE DISTINCT LISTS OF ALL PERSONS VOTED FOR AS PRESIDENT, AND OF ALL PERSONS VOTED FOR AS VICE-PRESIDENT, AND OF THE NUMBER OF VOTES FOR EACH, WHICH LISTS THEY SHALL SIGN AND CERTIFY, AND TRANSMIT SEALED TO THE SEAT OF THE GOVERNMENT OF THE UNITED STATES, DIRECTED TO THE PRESIDENT OF THE SENATE;—THE PRESIDENT OF THE SENATE SHALL, IN THE PRESENCE OF THE SENATE AND HOUSE OF REPRESENTATIVES, OPEN ALL CERTIFICATES AND THE VOTES SHALL THEN BE COUNTED;—THE PERSON HAVING THE GREATEST NUMBER OF VOTES FOR PRESIDENT, SHALL BE THE PRESIDENT, IF SUCH NUMBER BE A MAJORITY OF THE WHOLE NUMBER OF ELECTORS APPOINTED; AND IF NO PERSON HAVE SUCH MAJORITY, THEN FROM THE PERSONS HAVING THE HIGHEST NUMBERS NOT EXCEEDING THREE ON THE LIST OF THOSE VOTED FOR AS PRESIDENT, THE HOUSE OF REPRESENTA-

TIVES SHALL CHOOSE IMMEDIATELY, BY BALLOT, THE
PRESIDENT. BUT IN CHOOSING THE PRESIDENT, THE VOTES
SHALL BE TAKEN BY STATES, THE REPRESENTATION FROM
EACH STATE HAVING ONE VOTE; A QUORUM FOR THIS PUR-
POSE SHALL CONSIST OF A MEMBER OR MEMBERS FROM
TWO-THIRDS OF THE STATES, AND A MAJORITY OF ALL THE
STATES SHALL BE NECESSARY TO A CHOICE. AND IF THE
HOUSE OF REPRESENTATIVES SHALL NOT CHOOSE A PRESI-
DENT WHENEVER THE RIGHT OF CHOICE SHALL DEVOLVE
UPON THEM, BEFORE THE FOURTH DAY OF MARCH NEXT
FOLLOWING, THEN THE VICE-PRESIDENT SHALL ACT AS
PRESIDENT, AS IN THE CASE OF THE DEATH OR OTHER
CONSTITUTIONAL DISABILITY OF THE PRESIDENT. THE PER-
SON HAVING THE GREATEST NUMBER OF VOTES AS VICE-
PRESIDENT, SHALL BE THE VICE-PRESIDENT, IF SUCH
NUMBER BE A MAJORITY OF THE WHOLE NUMBER OF
ELECTORS APPOINTED, AND IF NO PERSON HAVE A MA-
JORITY, THEN FROM THE TWO HIGHEST NUMBERS ON THE
LIST, THE SENATE SHALL CHOOSE THE VICE-PRESIDENT;
A QUORUM FOR THE PURPOSE SHALL CONSIST OF TWO-
THIRDS OF THE WHOLE NUMBER OF SENATORS, AND A MA-
JORITY OF THE WHOLE NUMBER SHALL BE NECESSARY TO
A CHOICE. BUT NO PERSON CONSTITUTIONALLY INELI-
GIBLE TO THE OFFICE OF PRESIDENT SHALL BE ELIGIBLE
TO THAT OF VICE-PRESIDENT OF THE UNITED STATES.

The underlined portion of this Amendment has been superseded by the Twentieth Amendment (see page 134).

The presidential electoral system is the classic example of how
custom and usage have amended and democratized the Constitution. As previously mentioned (see pages 41–43), the authors of
the Constitution expected electors to be distinguished citizens
who would in fact, as well as in form, choose the President and
Vice-President. Their expectations did not materialize because of
the rise of national political parties. By the election of 1800 electors had come to be party puppets, pledged in advance to vote
for the candidates nominated by their respective parties. In this

election the Republican-Democratic electors were in a majority; but since under the original provisions for selecting the President and Vice-President each elector voted for two individuals without indicating which was his choice for President and which for Vice-President. Aaron Burr, the Republican-Democratic candidate for Vice-President, secured the same number of electoral votes as did Thomas Jefferson, the Republican-Democratic candidate for President. This circumstance transferred the election to the House of Representatives, where the Federalists were in control. Although many Federalists favored Burr as the lesser of two evils, Hamilton threw his great influence on the side of Jefferson, who was finally elected on the thirty-sixth ballot. Amendment XII was designed to prevent such a situation from occurring again.

The two major differences between the Twelfth Amendment and the original provisions of the Constitution which were repealed by it are as follows: today electors are required to cast separate votes for President and Vice-President, clearly designating which is their choice for President and which for Vice-President. In the event no person receives a majority of the electoral votes for President, the House of Representatives chooses from the three persons with the most electoral votes (original provision was from the five highest). If no person receives a majority of the electoral vote for Vice-President, the Senate chooses between the two persons with the most electoral votes.

Today presidential and vice-presidential candidates are chosen by political parties in national nominating conventions. On the first Tuesday after the first Monday in November the voters select the electors, who are morally pledged to cast their electoral votes for the candidates chosen by their particular national convention. In some states the electors' names do not even appear on the ballot, but only the names of the candidates to whom they are pledged. Thus the electors have been reduced to automata and "the Electoral College," as the electors are known collectively, to an automatic registering device (but see page 112).

The development of the two-party system had another consequence for the Electoral College which the framers did not anticipate. It greatly lessened the probability that the House of Representatives would be called upon to make the final selection. Only once since 1801 has the House exercised this duty. In the election of 1824, before the full development of our party system, Andrew Jackson, John Quincy Adams, and William Crawford received the most electoral votes, but not one of them had a majority. The House, voting by states, chose John Quincy Adams. The only time the Senate has been called upon to make the final selection for the vice-presidency was in 1837 when it favored Richard M. Johnson over Francis Granger. With only two major political parties there is no dispersion of the vote and one party is assured of a majority of the electoral votes. Should, however, a strong third party develop, the probability of final selection by the House and Senate would be greatly increased.

All the state legislatures now provide for the selection of electors on a general state-wide straight-ticket basis. Each voter casts one vote for the Democratic, or the Republican, or the Socialist, etc. electors. This means that the party which receives the most popular votes in a state receives *all* of that state's electoral votes. For example, in 1948 Dewey (i.e., the Republican electors) received 1,445,584 votes in Ohio and Truman received 1,452,791, a modest majority of 7,107 votes; nevertheless President Truman received all twenty-five of Ohio's electoral votes. It is even possible for a person to receive a majority of the popular vote without receiving a majority of the electoral vote. Let us take a hypothetical case involving two states to illustrate this point:

State X—15 electoral votes—Republican popular votes 255,000
Democratic popular votes 250,000

State Y— 5 electoral votes—Republican popular votes 20,000
Democratic popular votes 50,000

Results: Republican popular vote—275,000—Republican electoral vote 15
Democratic popular vote—300,000—Democratic electoral vote 5

This very thing happened in 1876 when Tilden received more popular votes but lost the electoral vote to Hayes, and again in 1888 when Cleveland, despite his larger popular vote, was defeated by Harrison.

The present system strengthens a one-party domination in Maine, Vermont, and the Southern states. In Mississippi, for example, the Republican party cannot hope to win the electoral votes because it can never secure a larger popular vote than the Democratic party. As anything less than a plurality would not count, the Republican party makes no great effort to get popular votes in Mississippi. Were, however, the President elected by a direct vote of the people or were electoral votes distributed in proportion to the popular vote, a Republican vote in Mississippi would be just as important as a Republican vote elsewhere, and there would be an incentive for the Republicans to campaign throughout the United States.

The threat of some electors to ignore the popular vote in the 1944 and 1948 elections, and the prospect at one time that the 1948 election might have to be decided by the House of Representatives, have increased the demands for abolishing the Electoral College. There is little likelihood of substituting direct popular election, however, because of the opposition of the less populous states. Since states have as many electoral votes as they have senators and representatives, the smaller states carry greater weight in the Electoral College than they would in a nation-wide direct election. Those who propose to do away with the Electoral College but retain the system of electoral votes and distribute a state's electoral vote in the same ratio as its popular vote, have a much better chance of success. Such a proposed amendment is now before Congress. The change would obviate any danger of electors' disregarding the wishes of the voters, lessen the influence of strategically located minorities, weaken the one-party system where it now exists, and ensure the election of the candidate with the largest popular vote.

Civil War Amendments

The Thirteenth, Fourteenth, and Fifteenth Amendments were adopted after and as a result of the Civil War. Their purpose was to free the Negro slaves, grant them citizenship, and protect their rights (especially the right to vote) against infringement by the states.

Amendment XIII—Slavery

Proposed January 31, 1865—Declared in force by the Secretary
of State December 18, 1865

Section 1

NEITHER SLAVERY NOR INVOLUNTARY SERVITUDE, EX-
CEPT AS A PUNISHMENT FOR CRIME WHEREOF THE PARTY
SHALL HAVE BEEN DULY CONVICTED, SHALL EXIST
WITHIN THE UNITED STATES, OR ANY PLACE SUBJECT
TO THEIR JURISDICTION.

Before the adoption of this Amendment each state could determine for itself whether or not slavery should be permitted within
its borders. This Amendment deprived both the states and the
national government of that power.

The Amendment was aimed at Negro slavery. Persons may
still be compelled to serve on a jury, in the militia, or in the armed
forces; to help build the public roads* or to pay alimony, all
without violating the Amendment.

Held to be contrary to the Thirteenth Amendment have been
several state laws which made failure to work after receiving
money prima-facie evidence of intent to defraud. In effect these
laws made it a crime punishable by imprisonment to fail to work
after securing money on the promise to do so.[19]

Amendment XIII is one of the two provisions of the Constitution (the other is the Twenty-first Amendment, see page 137),

---

* Under the common law men could be drafted for a certain number of days
every year for this purpose. In some cases payment of taxes exempted them
from such duties.

which a private individual can violate directly. It is, in other words, "self-executing"; that is, it does not require action by Congress to put it into effect, although in fact Congress has implemented it and attached penalties to its violation.

Section 2

CONGRESS SHALL HAVE POWER TO ENFORCE THIS ARTICLE BY APPROPRIATE LEGISLATION.

Amendment XIV—Citizenship, Privileges and Immunities of United States Citizenship, Due Process of the Law

Proposed June 13, 1866—Declared in force by the Secretary of State July 20, 1868

Section 1

1. ALL PERSONS BORN OR NATURALIZED IN THE UNITED STATES, AND SUBJECT TO THE JURISDICTION THEREOF, ARE CITIZENS OF THE UNITED STATES AND OF THE STATE WHEREIN THEY RESIDE.

This clause reversed the Dred Scott decision whereby United States citizenship was denied to Negroes both free and enslaved. Persons born in the United States but not subject to the jurisdiction thereof are: children of foreign diplomats and children born of alien enemies in the event of a hostile occupation of the United States.* All other children born in the United States become citizens even though their parents are aliens who are ineligible for citizenship.

---

* Although the Indian tribes are subject to the jurisdiction of the United States, they have been considered in a special category, as "wards of the nation" and the Fourteenth Amendment did not directly confer citizenship upon them. However, all Indians are now citizens of the United States by act of Congress.

While the clause confers citizenship on the principle of *jus soli*—by reason of place of birth—it does not prevent Congress from conferring citizenship by *jus sanguinis*—by reason of blood. For example, by law of Congress children born outside of the United States to American citizens are citizens of the United States "from birth." Citizenship may also be acquired by naturalization (see page 26).

Section 1

1. continued: NO STATE SHALL MAKE OR ENFORCE ANY LAW WHICH SHALL ABRIDGE THE PRIVILEGES OR IMMUNITIES OF CITIZENS OF THE UNITED STATES;

The primary purpose of this and the following sections was, originally, to confer upon the national government the power to protect the civil and political rights of the freedmen. Had the Amendment been carried out as intended, it would have produced a fundamental change in the nature of our federal system, for it would have given the national government jurisdiction over the entire realm of civil rights. In face of the intent of the Amendment, however, the Supreme Court, feeling that its authors did not realize the consequences with which their handiwork was fraught, interpreted the above clause in such a way as to prevent any significant change. In the very first case in which the Fourteenth Amendment came before it, the Court held that there are two distinct citizenships, state and federal, and that the "fundamental" civil and political rights which we enjoy are "privileges and immunities" stemming from *state*, not *United States* citizenship. In other words, this clause of the Fourteenth Amendment conferred no new rights upon United States citizens, but merely made explicit a federal guarantee against state abridgment of already established rights.[20]

The privileges and immunities of *United States* citizenship (which this Amendment forbids the states to abridge) are those which owe their existence to the national government, the Constitution, and the laws and treaties of the United States, like the right of ingress and egress to and from the states, the right to visit the national capital, the right to engage in interstate and foreign commerce, the right to protection on the high seas and in foreign countries, the right to vote in primaries and general elections in which congressmen are chosen and to have that vote properly counted, etc. On the other hand, the Court has held that the following are *not* privileges or immunities of United States citizens: the right to be secure in one's home, the right to exemption from unreasonable searches and seizures by *state* authorities, the right to refuse to give self-incriminatory evidence in *state* courts, the right to attend public schools, the right to engage in a legal occupation, the right to vote in state elections and to hold *state* office, and the right to trial by jury cases prosecuted by a *state*.[21] But while these are not privileges of *United States* citizens as such, many of them are today protected by the "due process" and "equal protection" clauses of Amendment XIV, as will be seen in a moment (see page 119).

Section 1

> 1. continued: NOR SHALL ANY STATE DEPRIVE ANY PERSON OF LIFE, LIBERTY, OR PROPERTY, WITHOUT DUE PROCESS OF LAW;

It should be emphasized that this clause, the "privileges and immunities" clause, and the "equal protection of laws" clause (see immediately below) are directed to the states, their officials, and local governments. Private wrongs—wrongful acts of private individuals—if not sanctioned in some way by a state, do not violate the Fourteenth Amendment. In brief, the Fourteenth Amendment protects individuals against *state*, not *private* action.

After the Supreme Court's interpretation of the "privileges and immunities" clause (see immediately above) rendered it ineffective as a protector of the "fundamental" rights, an attempt was made to make the "due process" clause serve this purpose. For many years it was argued that civil liberties were part of the "liberty" which the Fourteenth Amendment safeguarded against deprivation by the states, but the Court rejected the contention, although it interpreted "liberty" so as to protect economic interests (see pages 98–99). But beginning in 1925 the Court expanded the interpretation of "liberty" to include liberty of speech, press, worship, assembly, and petition.[22] Hence all the rights which are protected by the First Amendment against interference by the national government are now deemed by the Court to be protected by the Fourteenth Amendment against interference by the states (see page 87).

Indeed, four members of the present Supreme Court (Justices Black, Douglas, Murphy, and Rutledge) contend that the "due process" clause of the Fourteenth Amendment requires the states to follow precisely the same procedures in criminal cases that the federal government is required to follow by the Fourth, Fifth, Sixth, and Eighth Amendments, but a majority of the Court, backed by many past decisions, hold otherwise.[23] The states, they contend, may use other procedures than those outlined in the Bill of Rights so long as they are not arbitrary and shocking to the sense of justice of the civilized world, a view which makes it necessary for the Court to decide each case on its merits. Proceeding in this way, the Court has held that involuntary confessions cannot be used to secure convictions; that third-degree methods are repugnant to the "due process" clause, that due process of law requires some sort of public trial; that in a trial by jury, the jury must be impartial and the accused must be informed of the charges against him. Any procedure omitting such safeguards would not be fair and just and would therefore be a denial of due process of law. Whether state courts must provide compulsory processes for obtaining witnesses for the defendant, for requiring witnesses against him to appear, or for making sure that he has the assistance of counsel depends, on the other hand, upon the circumstances of the particular case. A state court can conceivably modify these requirements and still achieve a fair and just trial. Likewise, states may place a person in jeopardy twice, require him to testify against himself, indict him by procedures other than a grand jury, and try him by a jury of less than twelve without necessarily denying him due process of the law.[24]

Section 1

1. continued: NOR DENY TO ANY PERSON WITHIN ITS JURISDICTION THE EQUAL PROTECTION OF THE LAWS.

This clause does not forbid states to make "reasonable" classifications which affect alike all persons similarly situated; but it does rule out "unreasonable" and "arbitrary" classifications, and especially such as are the outgrowth of racial or religious animosities. Thus, a California statute forbidding the issuance of a commercial fishing license to aliens ineligible for citizenship (in other words Japanese) was recently held to violate the constitutional right of aliens to equal protection of the laws.[25] Since there is no "equal protection" clause limiting the national government (although the "due process" clause prevents grossly discriminatory legislation), its classifications are not subject to as close judicial scrutiny as are those made by the states.

Despite the "equal protection" clause, a state may require racial segregation; but if it does so it must provide equal public facilities. For example, if a state supports a law school for Caucasians, Negroes must either be allowed to attend it or be afforded equally good facilities elsewhere within the state.[26] Although the Supreme Court cannot accomplish the impossible, yet within recent years it has not permitted mere formal compliance with the constitutional requirement of equality to blind it to the more subtle forms of state discrimination. Thus, by a recent decision, while private individuals may place restrictive covenants in deeds, that is, agreements whereby the sale or use of the property is restricted to certain groups, such covenants, when based on racial grounds, may not be enforced by state courts, since that would be a denial of equal protection aided and abetted by the state.[27]

Any indictment or conviction of a Negro by a jury from which Negroes have been excluded because of their race, whether by law or by official action, is without force because it is a denial by the state of equal protection of the laws.*[28] On the

---

* Nevertheless, when court officials saw to it that one and only one Negro was placed on a grand jury, the Supreme Court found no violation of the equal protection clause (see note 28).

other hand, the indictment or conviction of a woman by a jury from which women have been excluded is not, necessarily, such a denial. And the Supreme Court lately refused to hold unconstitutional New York's "blue ribbon" (specially chosen) juries, no connection having been shown to exist between such juries and discrimination against any race, class, or occupation.[29] (See also page 100 above.)

Section 2

1. REPRESENTATIVES SHALL BE APPORTIONED AMONG THE SEVERAL STATES ACCORDING TO THEIR RESPECTIVE NUMBERS, COUNTING THE WHOLE NUMBER OF PERSONS IN EACH STATE, EXCLUDING INDIANS NOT TAXED.

This section supersedes Article I, Section 2, paragraph 3. Slaves were originally counted at three fifths of the number of free persons. At the present time all persons are counted in apportioning representatives since all Indians are now subject to taxation.

Section 2

1. continued: BUT WHEN THE RIGHT TO VOTE AT ANY ELECTION FOR THE CHOICE OF ELECTORS FOR PRESIDENT AND VICE PRESIDENT OF THE UNITED STATES, REPRESENTATIVES IN CONGRESS, THE EXECUTIVE AND JUDICIAL OFFICERS OF A STATE, OR THE MEMBERS OF THE LEGISLATURE THEREOF, IS DENIED TO ANY OF THE MALE INHABITANTS OF SUCH STATE, BEING TWENTY-ONE YEARS OF AGE, AND CITIZENS OF THE UNITED STATES, OR IN ANY WAY ABRIDGED, EXCEPT FOR PARTICIPATION IN REBELLION, OR OTHER CRIME, THE BASIS OF REPRESENTATION THEREIN SHALL BE REDUCED IN THE PROPORTION WHICH THE NUMBER OF SUCH MALE CITIZENS SHALL BEAR TO THE WHOLE NUMBER OF MALE CITIZENS TWENTY-ONE YEARS OF AGE IN SUCH STATE.

This provision has never been enforced by Congress, and may today be regarded as obsolete through disuse; also, possibly, because of its obvious disharmony with Amendment XIX (see page 132).

Section 3

NO PERSON SHALL BE A SENATOR OR REPRESENTATIVE IN CONGRESS, OR ELECTOR OF PRESIDENT AND VICE PRESIDENT, OR HOLD ANY OFFICE, CIVIL OR MILITARY, UNDER THE UNITED STATES, OR UNDER ANY STATE, WHO, HAVING PREVIOUSLY TAKEN AN OATH, AS A MEMBER OF CONGRESS, OR AS AN OFFICER OF THE UNITED STATES, OR AS A MEMBER OF ANY STATE LEGISLATURE, OR AS AN EXECUTIVE OR JUDICIAL OFFICER OF ANY STATE, TO SUPPORT THE CONSTITUTION OF THE UNITED STATES, SHALL HAVE ENGAGED IN INSURRECTION OR REBELLION AGAINST THE SAME, OR GIVEN AID OR COMFORT TO THE ENEMIES THEREOF. BUT CONGRESS MAY BY A VOTE OF TWO-THIRDS OF EACH HOUSE, REMOVE SUCH DISABILITY.

This section politically disabled those who led the Southern states into the Confederacy. It was placed in the Amendment by the radical Republicans and was a factor in their struggle with President Johnson. It limited the President's power to pardon the leaders of the Confederacy and thus restore them to citizenship. Congress removed this disability on June 6, 1898.

Section 4

THE VALIDITY OF THE PUBLIC DEBT OF THE UNITED STATES, AUTHORIZED BY LAW, INCLUDING DEBTS INCURRED FOR PAYMENT OF PENSIONS AND BOUNTIES FOR SERVICES IN SUPPRESSING INSURRECTION OR REBELLION, SHALL NOT BE QUESTIONED. BUT NEITHER THE UNITED STATES NOR ANY STATE SHALL ASSUME OR PAY ANY DEBT OR OBLIGATION INCURRED IN AID OF INSURRECTION OR REBELLION AGAINST THE UNITED STATES, OR ANY CLAIM FOR THE LOSS OR EMANCIPATION OF ANY SLAVE; BUT

ALL SUCH DEBTS, OBLIGATIONS AND CLAIMS SHALL BE
HELD ILLEGAL AND VOID.

This section invalidated all the securities and other evidences of debt of the Confederacy, while it reaffirmed those of the Union.

Section 5

THE CONGRESS SHALL HAVE POWER TO ENFORCE, BY AP-
PROPRIATE LEGISLATION, THE PROVISIONS OF THIS
ARTICLE.

As a result of the limited interpretation which the Supreme Court gave to the "privileges and immunities" clause of Section 1, the power of Congress under the above section is limited to the prevention or correction of state denials of life, liberty, and property without due process of the law, or of equal protection of the laws. For example, when Congress made it a federal offense for any innkeeper to deny accommodations to any person because of his race or color, the Supreme Court held that this was beyond the powers of Congress since it was an attempt to control *private* rather than *state* discrimination.[30] Independently of this section, however, Congress has power to protect the privileges and immunities of United States citizens from both private and state interference, and has done so by making it a crime to conspire willfully to deprive any United States citizen of any rights which he possesses by virtue of the federal Constitution or of federal law.[31]

Amendment XV—The Right to Vote

Proposed February 26, 1869—Declared in force by the Secretary of State March 30, 1870

Section 1

THE RIGHT OF CITIZENS OF THE UNITED STATES TO VOTE SHALL NOT BE DENIED OR ABRIDGED BY THE UNITED STATES OR BY ANY STATE ON ACCOUNT OF RACE, COLOR, OR PREVIOUS CONDITION OF SERVITUDE.

Despite this Amendment many Negroes are prevented from voting by ingenious methods devised to circumvent it; this is especially true in the Southern states. Qualifications for voting have been established which on their face are not discriminatory, but which have the actual effect of denying Negroes the right to vote. For example, in seven states one must pay a poll tax in order to vote. While this is prohibitive for many whites, Negro voters, many of whom are in depressed circumstances, are especially affected. In some states the taxes are cumulative, and the back taxes amount to a substantial sum for those whose cash income per year is only a few hundred dollars. Some states require the presentation of poll tax receipts at the time of voting in the hope that through carelessness and as a result of their migratory habits many Negroes will have lost their receipts by voting time. Stiff residence requirements have been adopted in certain states in the expectation that they will disqualify many Negroes. Other technicalities, such as registration during the year prior to the election, prevent many uneducated Negroes, and whites as well, from casting their ballot. Since none of these restrictions directly discriminate against Negroes, it is difficult to demonstrate judicially that their purpose is to keep them from voting.

But since most of these methods also prevent many whites from voting, other devices have been concocted at times. Among the first used was the "grandfather clause." This provided for a literacy test, but exempted all persons whose ancestors had the vote before January 1, 1866. Since no Negroes could vote at that time, while whites could, this was held to be a direct violation of the Fifteenth Amendment. As Justice Frankfurter pointed out in a similar case, "The Fifteenth Amendment nullifies sophisticated as well as simple-minded modes of discrimination."[32]

Another discriminatory scheme was the "white primary." In the Southern states the only politically effective party is the Democratic party, and the only effective election is the Democratic primary, the winner of which invariably wins the general election. Operating on the theory that the Democratic party was a private organization, its officials denied Negroes the right to vote in the Democratic primary. The Supreme Court, however, took a different view: "When primaries [it said] become a part of the machinery for choosing officials . . . , the same tests to determine the character of discrimination . . . should be applied to the primary as are applied to the general election." The Court pointed out, too, that state election officials enforced the decisions of the primary, and gave the primary nominees a preferred position on the election ballot. "The State," said the Court, "endorses, adopts and enforces the discrimination against Negroes, practiced by a party entrusted . . . by law with the determination of the qualifications of participants in the primary. This is State action within the meaning of the Fifteenth Amendment."[33] South Carolina thereupon repealed all of her laws referring in any way to primaries or parties; but the United States Circuit Court has ruled subsequently that this was merely a subterfuge to circumvent the Supreme Court's decision, and in no way affected the basic nature of the party primary. The case is now on its way to the Supreme Court.

Some modes of discrimination against the Negro voter have, however, eluded the Amendment. For instance, tests that require the voter to demonstrate comprehension of the Constitution are often administered by election officials in such a way that all whites pass and all Negroes fail; and literacy tests are often manipulated in the same way.

Amendment XV forcefully demonstrates that the Supreme Court, sitting in Washington, cannot by itself invariably protect the rights guaranteed by the Constitution. Nevertheless, within the last several years the Court has taken the lead in bringing action into closer conformity with the letter and spirit of the Fifteenth Amendment. In the future it will be more difficult than in the past for states to abridge the right to vote because of color.

Section 2

THE CONGRESS SHALL HAVE POWER TO ENFORCE THIS ARTICLE BY APPROPRIATE LEGISLATION.

Amendment XVI—Income Taxes

Proposed July 12, 1909—Declared in force by the Secretary of
State February 25, 1913

THE CONGRESS SHALL HAVE POWER TO LAY AND COLLECT
TAXES ON INCOMES, FROM WHATEVER SOURCE DERIVED,
WITHOUT APPORTIONMENT AMONG THE SEVERAL STATES,
AND WITHOUT REGARD TO ANY CENSUS OR ENUMERATION.

During the Civil War an income tax was levied as part of the
war financing program. As was generally expected, the Supreme
Court upheld the national government's right to levy such a tax.
In 1894 the Wilson-Gorham Tariff levied a 2 per cent tax on incomes over $4,000. The year following, after hearing the tax
assailed as the opening wedge of "Populism," "Communism,"
and the like, the Supreme Court held, by a five-to-four decision,
that a tax on income from property was tantamount to a tax on
the property itself, and hence a "direct tax" which had to be apportioned among the several states according to population
(Article 1, Section 2, paragraph 3, see page 6).[34] The levying of an income tax was thus rendered impracticable until the
adoption of the above Amendment in 1913.

Amendment XVII—Direct Election of United States Senators

Proposed May 13, 1912—Declared in force by the Secretary of State May 31, 1913

Section 1

> THE SENATE OF THE UNITED STATES SHALL BE COMPOSED OF TWO SENATORS FROM EACH STATE, ELECTED BY THE PEOPLE THEREOF, FOR SIX YEARS; AND EACH SENATOR SHALL HAVE ONE VOTE. THE ELECTORS IN EACH STATE SHALL HAVE THE QUALIFICATIONS REQUISITE FOR ELECTORS OF THE MOST NUMEROUS BRANCH OF THE STATE LEGISLATURES.

The adoption of universal suffrage and the growing strength of the democratic spirit made it inevitable that United States senators should be chosen directly by the people. During the last half of the nineteenth century the dissident labor and farmer parties had called for direct election. The revelation of certain senators' great wealth and of their obligations to various large economic interests reinforced these demands. By the turn of the century all the major parties supported proposals for direct election, the House of Representatives several times passed resolutions proposing an amendment to make the change, and finally in 1912 the Senate capitulated. As a matter of fact, by that date the voters in half of the states had obtained the right to indicate their preference for senator in the party primaries, and the state legislatures normally followed the wishes of the voters. The adoption of the Amendment merely rounded out a reform that had been long under way.

Section 2

WHEN VACANCIES HAPPEN IN THE REPRESENTATION OF ANY STATE IN THE SENATE, THE EXECUTIVE AUTHORITY OF SUCH STATE SHALL ISSUE WRITS OF ELECTION TO FILL SUCH VACANCIES: PROVIDED, THAT THE LEGISLATURE OF ANY STATE MAY EMPOWER THE EXECUTIVE THEREOF TO MAKE TEMPORARY APPOINTMENTS UNTIL THE PEO-PLE FILL THE VACANCIES BY ELECTION AS THE LEGIS-LATURE MAY DIRECT.

Most vacancies are filled by temporary appointments.

Section 3

THIS AMENDMENT SHALL NOT BE SO CONSTRUED AS TO AFFECT THE ELECTION OR TERM OF ANY SENATOR CHOSEN BEFORE IT BECOMES VALID AS PART OF THE CONSTITU-TION.

*Amendment XVIII—*Prohibition

Proposed December 18, 1917—Declared in force by the Acting
Secretary of State January 29, 1919

Section 1

> AFTER ONE YEAR FROM THE RATIFICATION OF THIS ARTI-
> CLE THE MANUFACTURE, SALE, OR TRANSPORTATION OF
> INTOXICATING LIQUORS WITHIN, THE IMPORTATION
> THEREOF INTO, OR THE EXPORTATION THEREOF FROM THE
> UNITED STATES AND ALL TERRITORY SUBJECT TO THE
> JURISDICTION THEREOF FOR BEVERAGE PURPOSES IS
> HEREBY PROHIBITED.

There have always been those who have waged war upon the
Demon Rum. As long ago as 1842 the state of Maine went dry,
and the Prohibition party has had a candidate in every presidential election since 1872. But it was the Anti-Saloon League—a
pressure group *de luxe,* formed in 1895—which gave the Prohibition movement its greatest impetus. During World War I
the necessity of saving grain lent Prohibition the guise of patriot-
ism. Although the above Amendment was ultimately ratified by
all of the states except Rhode Island and Connecticut, it always
lacked the support of large groups of citizens, especially in the
large cities. Bootlegging, lax enforcement, and general disregard
for the Amendment impaired regard for the entire Constitution.
The "noble experiment," as it was called, demonstrated that it is
almost impossible to regulate personal conduct by legal machinery when the law is contrary to the mores of large sections

of the country. National Prohibition was finally repealed in 1933 by the Twenty-first Amendment (see pages 137–138).

Section 2

THE CONGRESS AND THE SEVERAL STATES SHALL HAVE CONCURRENT POWER TO ENFORCE THIS ARTICLE BY AP-PROPRIATE LEGISLATION.

Section 3

THIS ARTICLE SHALL BE INOPERATIVE UNLESS IT SHALL HAVE BEEN RATIFIED AS AN AMENDMENT TO THE CON-STITUTION BY THE LEGISLATURES OF THE SEVERAL STATES, AS PROVIDED IN THE CONSTITUTION, WITHIN SEVEN YEARS FROM THE DATE OF THE SUBMISSION HEREOF TO THE STATES BY THE CONGRESS.

Amendment XIX—Women's Suffrage

Proposed June 4, 1919—Declared in force by the Secretary of State August 26, 1920

Section 1

THE RIGHT OF CITIZENS OF THE UNITED STATES TO VOTE SHALL NOT BE DENIED OR ABRIDGED BY THE UNITED STATES OR BY ANY STATE ON ACCOUNT OF SEX.

This Amendment was the culmination of a struggle beginning in the 1840's. In 1890 women were admitted to full suffrage rights in Wyoming, and by the time the Amendment was adopted fifteen states and Alaska had given them full suffrage, fourteen states had given them "presidential suffrage," and two states had given them the right to take part in the primaries. Many of the arguments advanced against women's suffrage sound ludicrous today. Much of the opposition came from certain business groups (especially the liquor industry) who feared that women would vote for regulation. Actually their votes have not materially changed our politics. Women began only gradually to exercise their right to vote, but with each election a greater percentage of eligible women are voting.

This Amendment does not affect state laws dealing with ownership of property, jury service, etc. Therefore many organizations are now advocating an "Equal-Rights Amendment" to confer upon women full equality with men. Such an Amendment was endorsed by the 1948 platforms of both major parties. Opponents of the proposed Amendment argue that it would jeopardize women's special privileges concerning hours of work, minimum wages, maternity benefits, etc.

Section 2

CONGRESS SHALL HAVE POWER TO ENFORCE THIS ARTICLE BY APPROPRIATE LEGISLATION.

Amendment XX—The Lame-Duck Amendment

Proposed March 3, 1932—Declared in force by the Secretary of State February 6, 1933

Section 1

THE TERMS OF THE PRESIDENT AND VICE PRESIDENT SHALL END AT NOON ON THE 20TH DAY OF JANUARY, AND THE TERMS OF SENATORS AND REPRESENTATIVES AT NOON ON THE 3RD DAY OF JANUARY, OF THE YEARS IN WHICH SUCH TERMS WOULD HAVE ENDED IF THIS ARTICLE HAD NOT BEEN RATIFIED; AND THE TERMS OF THEIR SUCCESSORS SHALL THEN BEGIN.

Before the adoption of this Amendment congressmen and the President elected in November did not take office until the following March, and newly elected congressmen did not (unless called into special session) actually get to legislate until the following December—thirteen months after their election. Meanwhile, congressmen defeated in the November elections ("lame-ducks") continued to serve until the following March 4, and although repudiated at the polls, continued to represent their constituencies in the December-to-March session.

Section 2

THE CONGRESS SHALL ASSEMBLE AT LEAST ONCE IN EVERY YEAR, AND SUCH MEETING SHALL BEGIN AT NOON ON THE

3RD DAY OF JANUARY, UNLESS THEY SHALL BY LAW
APPOINT A DIFFERENT DAY.

This section supersedes Article 1, Section 4, paragraph 2 (see page 12) which called for Congress to meet on the first Monday in December, and so necessitated every other year a short, ineffective December-to-March "lame-duck" session. The Twentieth Amendment does away with this session, which was frequently featured in the Senate by filibusters.

Section 3

IF, AT THE TIME FIXED FOR THE BEGINNING OF THE TERM
OF THE PRESIDENT, THE PRESIDENT ELECT SHALL HAVE
DIED, THE VICE PRESIDENT ELECT SHALL BECOME PRESI-
DENT. IF A PRESIDENT SHALL NOT HAVE BEEN CHOSEN
BEFORE THE TIME FIXED FOR THE BEGINNING OF HIS
TERM, OR IF THE PRESIDENT ELECT SHALL HAVE FAILED
TO QUALIFY, THEN THE VICE PRESIDENT ELECT SHALL
ACT AS PRESIDENT UNTIL A PRESIDENT SHALL HAVE
QUALIFIED; AND THE CONGRESS MAY BY LAW PROVIDE
FOR THE CASE WHEREIN NEITHER A PRESIDENT ELECT
NOR A VICE PRESIDENT ELECT SHALL HAVE QUALIFIED,
DECLARING WHO SHALL THEN ACT AS PRESIDENT, OR THE
MANNER IN WHICH ONE WHO IS TO ACT SHALL BE SE-
LECTED, AND SUCH PERSON SHALL ACT ACCORDINGLY
UNTIL A PRESIDENT OR VICE PRESIDENT SHALL HAVE
QUALIFIED.

It should be noted that within the meaning of the Constitution there is no President-elect or Vice-President-elect until the electoral votes have been counted by Congress or, in the event that no person has a majority of the electoral votes, until the House of Representatives and the Senate make their choice.

Congress has now made the same provision for succession in the event of the disability, or disqualification of the President-*elect* and the Vice-President-*elect*, as in the case of the President and Vice-President (see pages 45–46).[35]

Section 4

THE CONGRESS MAY BY LAW PROVIDE FOR THE CASE OF THE DEATH OF ANY OF THE PERSONS FROM WHOM THE HOUSE OF REPRESENTATIVES MAY CHOOSE A PRESIDENT WHENEVER THE RIGHT OF CHOICE SHALL HAVE DE-VOLVED UPON THEM, AND FOR THE CASE OF THE DEATH OF ANY OF THE PERSONS FROM WHOM THE SENATE MAY CHOOSE A VICE PRESIDENT WHENEVER THE RIGHT OF CHOICE SHALL HAVE DEVOLVED UPON THEM.

Congress has failed to act under this section.

Section 5

SECTIONS 1 AND 2 SHALL TAKE EFFECT ON THE 15TH DAY OF OCTOBER FOLLOWING THE RATIFICATION OF THIS ARTICLE.

Section 6

THIS ARTICLE SHALL BE INOPERATIVE UNLESS IT SHALL HAVE BEEN RATIFIED AS AN AMENDMENT TO THE CON-STITUTION BY THE LEGISLATURES OF THREE-FOURTHS OF THE SEVERAL STATES WITHIN SEVEN YEARS FROM THE DATE OF ITS SUBMISSION.

Amendment XXI—Repeal of Prohibition

Proposed February 20, 1933—Declared in force by the
Secretary of State December 5, 1933

Section 1

THE EIGHTEENTH ARTICLE OF AMENDMENT TO THE CON-
STITUTION OF THE UNITED STATES IS HEREBY REPEALED.

It soon became apparent that the Eighteenth Amendment, in-
stead of diminishing the amount of liquor consumed, actually
diverted taxes and profits from legitimate interests into the hands
of bootleggers and criminals and was endangering respect for the
Constitution and the laws of the land. The demand for repeal
became insistent. In 1928 Alfred Smith, the Democratic candidate for President, advocated repeal, and by 1932 the platforms
of both major parties were, in the phrase of the day "dripping
wet."

Section 2

THE TRANSPORTATION OR IMPORTATION INTO ANY STATE,
TERRITORY, OR POSSESSION OF THE UNITED STATES FOR
DELIVERY OR USE THEREIN OF INTOXICATING LIQUORS, IN
VIOLATION OF THE LAWS THEREOF, IS HEREBY PRO-
HIBITED.

Just as some areas of the country resented prohibition, so
others, mainly rural, wished to retain it. This section aids them

in doing so. But their regulations to this end must be "reasonable" in the judgment of the Court, and may be set aside by Congress under the "commerce" clause.

Section 3

THIS ARTICLE SHALL BE INOPERATIVE UNLESS IT SHALL HAVE BEEN RATIFIED AS AN AMENDMENT TO THE CONSTITUTION BY CONVENTIONS IN THE SEVERAL STATES, AS PROVIDED IN THE CONSTITUTION, WITHIN SEVEN YEARS FROM THE DATE OF THE SUBMISSION HEREOF TO THE STATES BY CONGRESS.

Proposed Amendments—Articles of Amendment Proposed by Congress Awaiting Ratification

Child Labor Amendment Proposed June 2, 1924

Section 1

THE CONGRESS SHALL HAVE POWER TO LIMIT, REGULATE, AND PROHIBIT THE LABOR OF PERSONS UNDER 18 YEARS OF AGE.

Section 2

THE POWER OF THE SEVERAL STATES IS UNIMPAIRED BY THIS ARTICLE EXCEPT THAT THE OPERATIONS OF STATE LAWS SHALL BE SUSPENDED TO THE EXTENT NECESSARY TO GIVE EFFECT TO THE LEGISLATION ENACTED BY CONGRESS.

Twenty-eight states have ratified this Amendment, the latest being Kansas, Kentucky, Nevada, and New Mexico in 1937. There is some question whether it is still alive and whether subsequent ratifications would secure its adoption. If a sufficient number of ratifications are eventually secured, Congress, through its directions to the Secretary of State, will decide the point (see page 75).

In 1916 Congress closed the channels of interstate commerce

to products made by or with the aid of child labor, but the Supreme Court invalidated the law as an invasion of the reserved powers of the states[36] (see page 105). Congress then levied a tax on all products made by or with the aid of child labor, but again the Supreme Court said no.[37] Following these abortive attempts, Congress proposed the above Amendment.

The reversal of the above-mentioned decisions in 1941 (see page 105) has lessened the need for such an amendment.[38] Congress has already prohibited the production by or with the aid of child labor of goods intended for interstate shipment (see page 24).

Presidential Term of Office Proposed March 24, 1947

Section 1

NO PERSON SHALL BE ELECTED TO THE OFFICE OF THE PRESIDENT MORE THAN TWICE, AND NO PERSON WHO HAS HELD THE OFFICE OF PRESIDENT, OR ACTED AS PRESIDENT, FOR MORE THAN TWO YEARS OF A TERM TO WHICH SOME OTHER PERSON WAS ELECTED PRESIDENT SHALL BE ELECTED TO THE OFFICE OF THE PRESIDENT MORE THAN ONCE. BUT THIS ARTICLE SHALL NOT APPLY TO ANY PERSON HOLDING THE OFFICE OF PRESIDENT, OR ACTING AS PRESIDENT DURING THE TERM WITHIN WHICH THIS ARTICLE BECOMES OPERATIVE FROM HOLDING THE OFFICE OF PRESIDENT OR ACTING AS PRESIDENT DURING THE REMAINDER OF SUCH TERM.

Section 2

THIS ARTICLE SHALL BE INOPERATIVE UNLESS IT SHALL HAVE BEEN RATIFIED AS AN AMENDMENT TO THE CONSTITUTION BY THE LEGISLATURES OF THREE-FOURTHS OF THE SEVERAL STATES WITHIN SEVEN YEARS FROM THE DATE OF ITS SUBMISSION TO THE STATES BY CONGRESS.

Despite the fact that there has been very little discussion of this proposed Amendment, twenty-one states had ratified it by the end of 1948. In most instances the legislators who voted on ratification were chosen before the proposal was voted by Congress, and consequently without any reference to it.

Adoption of the proposal has been urged on the ground that it would put another obstacle in the path of a would-be dictator; that it would restore in a definite fashion "the wise unwritten rule" against a third term which was broken in 1940; that continuance of the same person in office longer than eight years strikes at the root of the principle of separation of powers, since the President may use his appointive powers to control the federal judiciary.

Arguments against adoption take the following line: That its proponents were animated by a partisan desire to strike at the reputation of President Franklin Roosevelt; that it is a reflection on the wisdom of the majority of voters; that a similar restriction was discussed and rejected by the Founding Fathers; that it places limitations upon the power of future generations, who will be more informed and more capable of deciding, in light of the requirements of the moment, whom to elect, than the people of this generation can possibly be.

Notes

The Preamble

1. McCulloch *v.* Maryland, 4 Wheaton 316 (1819). This citation means that this case can be located in the fourth volume of Wheaton's Supreme Court Reports on page 316, and that the case was decided in 1819. Cases that came to the Supreme Court after 1875 are cited by the number of the Supreme Court Report rather than by the name of the Supreme Court reporter. Thus the case of United States *v.* Lovett is cited 328 U.S. 303 (1946). In other words, the case can be found in the 328th volume of the United States Supreme Court Reports on page 303 and it was decided in 1946. Two other methods of citation are used, but the one described here is the most common.

Article I

1. The *Constitution of Massachusetts,* Part the First, Article XXX.
2. This maxim stems from Chapter XI of John Locke's famous *Second Treatise of Civil Government,* (Sherman, Charles L. edition, p. 95. New York: D. Appleton-Century Co., 1937).
3. Lichter *v.* United States, 334 U.S. 742 (1948).
4. United States *v.* Curtiss-Wright Export Corporation, 299 U.S. 304 (1936).
5. *Ex Parte* Yarbrough, 110 U.S. 651 (1884).
6. Galloway, George B., *Congress at the Crossroads,* p. 347. New York: Thomas Y. Crowell Co., 1946.
7. United States *v.* Classic, 313 U.S. 299 (1941); Smith *v.* Allwright, 321 U.S. 649 (1944).

8. McGrain v. Daugherty, 273 U.S. 135 (1927).
9. McCulloch v. Maryland, 4 Wheaton 316 (1819).
10. Gibbons v. Ogden, 9 Wheaton 1 (1824).
11. United States v. Darby, 312 U.S. 100 (1941).
12. United States v. Appalachian Electric Power Co., 311 U.S. 377 (1940).
13. Hennington v. Georgia, 163 U.S. 299 (1896).
14. Southern Pacific Co. v. Arizona, 325 U.S. 761 (1945).
15. The Minnesota Rate Cases, 230 U.S. 352, (1913).
16. For a fuller discussion see Corwin, Edward S., *The Constitution and What It Means Today*, (10th ed.), pp. 44–48. Princeton: Princeton University Press, 1948.
17. For a fuller discussion see Corwin, *op. cit.*, pp. 48ff.
18. Fong Yue Ting v. United States, 149 U.S. 698 (1893).
19. For fuller treatment of both these topics see Corwin, *op. cit.*, pp. 48–53.
20. Hughes, Charles Evans, "War Powers Under the Constitution," 42 *Reports of the American Bar Association*, September 5, 1917; Minnesota Mortgage Moratorium Case, 290 U.S. 398 (1934). For a fuller treatment of this subject see Corwin, Edward S., *Total War and the Constitution*. New York: Alfred K. Knopf, 1947.
21. For a fuller discussion see Corwin, *The Constitution and What It Means Today*, pp. 95–96, 163–164.
22. McCulloch v. Maryland, 4 Wheaton 316 (1819).
23. United States v. Lovett, 328 U.S. 303 (1946).
24. Fletcher v. Peck, 6 Cranch 87 (1810); Dartmouth College v. Woodward, 4 Wheaton 518 (1819); Sturges v. Crowinshield, 4 Wheaton 122 (1819).
25. Charles River Bridge Co. v. Warren Bridge, 11 Peters 420 (1837); Stone v. Mississippi, 101 U.S. 814 (1880).

Article II

1. For a fuller treatment of this Article see Corwin, Edward S., *The President's Office and Powers*, (3rd ed.). New York: New York University Press, 1948.
2. Locke, John, *Second Treatise*, p. 109.

3. Madison, James, *The Records of the Federal Convention of 1787*, edited by Farrand, Max, Volume II, p. 110. New Haven: Yale University Press, 1937.
4. Mason, George, *Records of Federal Convention*, Volume II, p. 31.
5. 3 U.S.C. 1, 7, 9–11, 15.
6. 3 U.S.C. 19.
7. Korematsu *v.* United States, 323 U.S. 214 (1944).
8. Duncan *v.* Kahanamoku, 327 U.S. 304 (1946).
9. For a fuller explanation see Corwin, *The Constitution and What It Means Today*, (10th ed.), pp. 99–106.
10. Myers *v.* United States, 272 U.S. 52 (1926); Humphrey's Executor *v.* United States, 295 U.S. 602 (1935).

Article III

1. Muskrat *v.* United States, 219 U.S. 346 (1911).
2. *Ex Parte* McCardle, 6 Wallace 318 (1868).
3. Holmes, Oliver Wendell, *Collected Legal Papers*, pp. 295–296. New York: Harcourt, Brace and Howe, 1920.

Article IV

1. Williams *v.* North Carolina, 325 U.S. 226 (1945).
2. Sherrer *v.* Sherrer, 324 U.S. 343 (1948). For a fuller treatment of this complex problem see Corwin, *The Constitution and What It Means Today*, pp. 135–137.
3. Toomer *v.* Witsell, 334 U.S. 385 (1948).
4. Compare Stearns *v.* Minnesota, 179 U.S. 223 (1900) with Coyle *v.* Smith, 221 U.S. 559 (1911).
5. Texas *v.* White, 7 Wallace 700 (1869).
6. Hawaii *v.* Mankichi, 190 U.S. 197 (1903); Balzac *v.* Porto Rico, 258 U.S. 298 (1922).
7. The Court made this summary of the decision in the Oregon case (Pacific States Telephone & Telegraph Co. *v.* Oregon, 223 U.S. 118 1912) in Colegrove *v.* Green, 328 U.S. 549 (1946).
8. Luther *v.* Borden, 7 Howard 1 (1849).
9. In re Debs, 158 U.S. 464 (1895).

Article V

1. Coleman *v.* Miller, 307 U.S. 433 (1939), concurring opinion.

Article VI

1. Hines *v.* Davidowitz, 312 U.S. 52 (1941).
2. Missouri *v.* Holland, 252 U.S. 416 (1920).

Article VII

No annotation.

Amendments

1. *The Federalists*, Number 84.
2. Cochran *v.* Louisiana State Board, 281 U.S. 370 (1930); Everson *v.* Board of Education, 330 U.S. 1 (1947).
3. McCollum *v.* Board of Education, 333 U.S. 703 (1948).
4. Lovell *v.* Griffin, 303 U.S. 44 (1938); Cantwell *v.* Connecticut, 301 U.S. 296 (1940); Murdock *v.* Pennsylvania, 319 U.S. 105 (1943); Martin *v.* Struthers, 319 U.S. 141 (1943). For a fuller discussion see Corwin, *The Constitution and What It Means Today*, (10th ed.), pp. 199–201.
5. Minersville School District *v.* Gobitis, 310 U.S. 586 (1940); West Virginia State Board of Education *v.* Barnette, 319 U.S. 624 (1943).
6. Schenck *v.* United States, 249 U.S. 47 (1919).
7. For a fuller treatment see Corwin, *op. cit.*, pp. 119, 156–159.
8. (Justice) Miller, Samuel F., *The Constitution*, p. 646 (1893) quoted in *The Constitution of The United States of America*, Senate Document 232, 74th Congress, 2d Session. Washington: Government Printing Office, 1938.
9. Johnson *v.* United States, 333 U.S. 10 (1948).
10. For a fuller account see Corwin, *op. cit.*, pp. 166–168.
11. Davidson *v.* New Orleans, 96 U.S. 97 (1878).
12. Winters *v.* New York, 333 U.S. 507 (1948).
13. Connally *v.* General Construction Co., 269 U.S. 385 (1926).
14. Meyers *v.* Nebraska, 262 U.S. 390 (1923).
15. For a fuller treatment see Corwin, *op. cit.*, pp. 168–175.
16. United States *v.* Butler, 297 U.S. 1 (1936).

17. United States *v.* Darby, 312 U.S. 100 (1941).
18. Chisholm *v.* Georgia, 2 Dallas 419 (1793).
19. Pollock *v.* Williams, 322 U.S. 4 (1944).
20. The Slaughterhouse Cases, 16 Wallace 36 (1873).
21. Twining *v.* New Jersey, 211 U.S. 78 (1908).
22. Gitlow *v.* New York, 268 U.S. 652 (1925).
23. Adams v. California, 322 U.S. 46 (1947), dissenting opinions.
24. For a fuller treatment see Corwin, *op. cit.*, pp. 188–207.
25. Takahaski *v.* Game Commission, 334 U.S. 410 (1948).
26. Missouri ex rel Gaines *v.* Canada, 305 U.S. 327 (1938).
27. Shelley *v.* Kraemer; McGhee *v.* Sipes, 334 U.S. 1 (1948).
28. Hill *v.* Texas, 310 U.S. 400 (1942); Akins *v.* Texas, 325 U.S. 398 (1945).
29. Fay *v.* New York, 332 U.S. 261 (1947).
30. The Civil Rights Cases, 109 U.S. 3 (1883).
31. 18 U.S.C. 51.
32. Lane *v.* Wilson, 307 U.S. 268 (1939).
33. Smith *v.* Allwright, 321 U.S. 649 (1944).
34. Pollock *v.* Farmers' Loan and Trust Co., 158 U.S. 601 (1895).
35. 3 U.S.C. 19.
36. Hammer *v.* Dagenhart, 247 U.S. 251 (1918).
37. Bailey *v.* Drexel Furniture Co. 259 U.S. 20 (1922).
38. United States *v.* Darby, 312 U.S. 100 (1941).